SOCIAL WELFARE POLICY AND SERVICES IN SOCIAL WORK EDUCATION

Social Welfare Policy and Services in Social Work Education

IRVING WEISSMAN

VOLUME XII

A Project Report of the Curriculum Study
Werner W. Boehm, Director and Coordinator

COUNCIL ON SOCIAL WORK EDUCATION
345 EAST 46TH STREET, NEW YORK 17, N. Y.

60
Printed in the United States of America
by H. Wolff Book Manufacturing Co., Inc.

PANEL PARTICIPANTS

The affiliations listed are those of the participants at the time of panel membership.

Chairman

Joseph P. Anderson
*National Association of Social
  Workers*
New York, New York

Martha Branscombe
Bureau of Social Affairs
United Nations
New York, New York

Wilbur J. Cohen
School of Social Work
University of Michigan
Ann Arbor, Michigan

Alice Taylor Davis
School of Social Work
Howard University
Washington, D.C.

Lyman S. Ford
*United Community Funds and
  Councils of America*
New York, New York

Henrietta L. Gordon
Child Welfare League of America
New York, New York

Gordon Hamilton
New York School of Social Work
Columbia University
New York, New York

Mary Houk
Division of Social Service
University of Indiana
Indianapolis, Indiana

Donald S. Howard
School of Social Welfare
University of California
Los Angeles, California

Dorothy M. Johnson
Veterans Administration
Washington, D.C.

Warren C. Lamson
National Institute of Mental Health
*Department of Health, Education,
  and Welfare*
Bethesda, Maryland

Arleigh L. Lincoln
*Raymond A. Kent School of Social
  Work*
University of Louisville
Louisville, Kentucky

John S. Morgan
School of Social Work
University of Toronto
Toronto, Ontario, Canada

Arthur Nebel
School of Social Work
University of Missouri
Columbia, Missouri

v

Ralph Ormsby
Family Service of Philadelphia
Philadelphia, Pennsylvania

Harold E. Simmons
Department of Public Health and
Welfare
San Mateo County, California

Will Turnbladh
National Probation and Parole
Association
New York, New York

Corinne H. Wolfe
Bureau of Public Assistance
Department of Health, Education,
and Welfare
Washington, D.C.

Project Director

Irving Weissman, M.S.W.
School of Social Work
Tulane University
New Orleans, Louisiana

Board Policy

This project report of the Curriculum Study is published in accordance with the policy adopted by the Board of Directors of the Council at its meeting on October 9–11, 1958. The policy adopted provides that:

The content of Curriculum Study reports are the responsibility of the Curriculum Study staff;

These reports will be published by the Council as submitted to it by the Study staff and given the widest possible distribution;

The Council, through all possible channels, shall encourage thorough consideration and discussion of the findings and recommendations and their implications for social work education and practice.

The Board decided further that:

Publication and distribution of the Curriculum Study reports does not imply Council acceptance of the findings or recommendations;

Implementation of any of the recommendations of the Study can come only after the field has had full opportunity to consider the reports, the appropriate bodies of the Council have considered and recommended action which would modify or change existing policies and standards.

The Board sincerely hopes that the many challenging questions which the Study presents will be given the mature, deliberate and objective consideration they merit and which characterize the true profession.

The Board wishes to register on behalf of the Council its sincere appreciation to the Study staff whose dedicated service brought the Curriculum Study to a successful conclusion.

The thirteen volumes of the Curriculum Study have been numbered to facilitate reference and identification. The comprehensive report has been numbered Volume I, the report on undergraduate education because of its comprehensive nature has been numbered Volume II. The other volumes have been numbered in alphabetical order by title as follows:

Acknowledgments

The Board is pleased to make public acknowledgment of its appreciation to the following foundations and organizations whose grants made possible the financing of this Curriculum Study:

FIELD FOUNDATION
ITTLESON FAMILY FOUNDATION
NATIONAL INSTITUTE OF MENTAL HEALTH, DEPARTMENT OF HEALTH, EDUCATION, AND WELFARE
NATIONAL TUBERCULOSIS ASSOCIATION
NEW YORK FUND FOR CHILDREN
OFFICE OF VOCATIONAL REHABILITATION, DEPARTMENT OF HEALTH, EDUCATION, AND WELFARE
ROCKEFELLER BROTHERS FUND

Although all projects of the Curriculum Study were interdependent and each contributed to the others and to the comprehensive report—and the staff worked as a team under one director—certain grants were more particularly earmarked for designated projects. Accordingly, acknowledgment is made of this circumstance in the appropriate volumes.

In addition to grants from these organizations, the Council on Social Work Education made substantial contributions from its own funds.

—Ernest F. Witte

New York, New York   *Executive Director*
May, 1959   *Council on Social Work Education*

viii

Preface

This comprehensive three-year study of curriculum in the education of social workers has been completed under the auspices of the Council on Social Work Education. It has comprised twelve separate projects, one of which is reported in the following pages.

The twelve individual project reports are published separately by the Council to meet the needs of social work educators and practitioners whose interest is especially concentrated in the subject matter of one or more of the projects. No single report, however, can be understood in its proper relation to the whole study without reference to the comprehensive report, *Objectives for the Social Work Curriculum of the Future,* in which the findings and recommendations of the total study are presented. The various project directors worked together as a staff under the over-all guidance of Dr. Werner W. Boehm, Director and Coordinator of the Curriculum Study. Their goal was not only to develop desirable educational objectives for each project's particular area of the curriculum or suggested by particular considerations of practice, but, in addition, to do so in a way that would merge them all into a total educational experience.

Each project was designed to fit into a master plan for the study of the total curriculum. The findings and recommendations of each are relevant to those of the whole Study and have in turn been influenced by all other projects. To be understood, each report must therefore be considered in relation to the comprehensive report, which it supplements by supplying details for the particular area of the social work curriculum.

WHY THE STUDY WAS UNDERTAKEN

Many issues facing social work education were identified in the Hollis-Taylor Report of 1951.[1] It confirmed that the great preponderance of persons engaged in social work activities were still without professional education. It raised such questions as:

Does social work have a well-defined and identified function?

Does it possess a systematic body of knowledge, skills and attitudes in the various areas of social work practice?

Is the content of social work education sufficiently well developed so that it can be transmitted, and is it of such caliber that it can be included properly as a professional discipline within a university?

Progress toward answering these questions was made by the adoption of the Council's Curriculum Policy Statement in 1952, but further study was indicated. Social work education had also to face other issues:

How could it meet the greatly increased need for social work personnel?

How best could it train for a professional practice still in the process of rapid change and development? Can it be broad enough in scope to enable social workers to function in fields just emerging as well as those already established? Will breadth of education to encompass all fields of professional practice result in dilution of competence for specific fields?

How could it inculcate qualities of leadership and statesmanship while at the same time training for competence in specific practice?

Should undergraduate education serve primarily as a basis for graduate training or also prepare personnel for certain social work positions?

The Study considered that materials from which answers to all these questions might emerge would be obtained by focusing upon

[1] Ernest V. Hollis and Alice L. Taylor, *Social Work Education in the United States* (New York: Columbia University Press, 1951).

fundamental questions of curriculum planning and not by piece-meal consideration of the specific questions posed. In education for social work as for other professions, the fundamental considerations in curriculum planning apply, as presented succinctly by Dr. Ralph W. Tyler.[2] Paraphrased for purposes of this study they are:

What are the desirable educational objectives for professional education?

What learning experiences should be selected and devised and how organized, to realize these objectives?

What are the effective means of evaluating whether the objectives have been attained?

Without a clear formulation of the objectives of social work education, that is, the knowledge, skills and attitudes students are expected to acquire, it becomes impossible to plan the learning experiences needed or to evaluate their success. Consequently, the Curriculum Study singled out as its major task identification of the desirable objectives of social work education.

Also, in accordance with Dr. Tyler's definition, each project framed its educational objectives in terms of both the *content* to be covered and the kind and quality of *behavior* to be expected from the student in relation to the content. For example, "familiarity" with a certain area of content becomes distinguishable from behaviors involving more complex manipulations or deeper "understanding" of content at other levels of student learning.

HOW THE STUDY WAS CARRIED ON

The individual projects of the study fell into the following major areas:

1. Specific curriculum areas—projects devised to examine the curriculum in the areas identified by the Curriculum Policy Statement of 1952: Human Growth and Behavior, the Social

2 Ralph W. Tyler, *Basic Principles of Curriculum and Instruction* (Chicago: The University of Chicago Press, 1950).

Services, Social Work Methods (casework, group work, community organization, research, administration).
2. Selected fields of practice—projects devised to study elements of practice in rehabilitation, public social services, and corrections.
3. Undergraduate education for social work.
4. Content on social work values and ethics found throughout the curriculum.

Each project was planned to identify educational objectives in existing curricula; to formulate a series of desirable objectives, the desirability of which was determined by judging their importance, consistency and compatibility with a statement of the nature and function of social work; and to review the objectives in the light of educational theory as to the possibility of their being learned in the time and conditions available. Project directors had consultation and assistance from specially selected panels of educators and practitioners in social work and related disciplines.

WHAT THE STUDY HOPES TO ACCOMPLISH

Responsibility for planning and constructing curriculum belongs basically to the social work schools and departments. As a group they have already come far toward definition of common educational goals for the profession and of content all curricula must have to reach such goals. The Curriculum Study is expected to provide guides for the resolution of the major issues and common questions that it is anticipated will arise in the curriculum planning of all member schools and departments of the Council on Social Work Education.

Contents

SOCIAL WELFARE POLICY AND
SERVICES IN SOCIAL
WORK EDUCATION

CHAPTER I

The Study Plan of the Project

This project is one part of a comprehensive study of social work curriculum. Its study design was developed within the framework of a central plan for the entire Curriclum Study. It has the same purpose and focus as all the other projects, namely, to define desirable objectives for professional education to serve as guides in curriculum-building for the member schools and departments of the Council on Social Work Education. It follows the common approach laid down by the central Study plan, which is based on the Tyler framework for identifying and formulating curriculum objectives. And, in methodology, it emphasizes the procedures outlined in the central plan for content analysis of collected materials and for the use of a panel of experts to review and advise on staff work.

The project's particular part in these common tasks was limited to one of the three major subject areas of the professional curriculum, the one designated "The Social Services" in the current *Curriculum Policy Statement* adopted by the Council on Social Work Education in 1952.[1]

CONDUCT OF THE PROJECT

Staff work on the project began in June 1956 with a preliminary survey and analysis of available data in the files of the Council on Social Work Education. Among the materials examined were reports of earlier curriculum studies, curriculum committee minutes and reports, school catalogs, and various other documents. After working through this material, a research plan for the project was formulated.[2]

1 Council on Social Work Education, *Curriculum Policy Statement* (New York: CSWE, 1952). Mimeographed.
2 This has been circulated as the *Research Plan for the Fields of Practice Project.* The term "Fields of Practice" was substituted for "Social Services" in the title of this project for a number of reasons. It was thought the new name would avoid confusion

The preliminary review of available materials provided an understanding of curriculum problems in teaching social services content and made it possible for the project to move quickly into its most time-consuming phase. This involved the selection and systematization of the content elements of the subject, which, with behavior elements, were to form statements of curriculum objectives.

Source materials were of two kinds. The first included such curricular materials as course outlines, syllabi, field work manuals, assignment and examination papers and course bibliographies. Schools furnished current materials of this sort in response to a general request for this kind of material for all projects. In this project, use was made principally of the materials from courses in this curriculum area which all students were required to take. It was believed that this procedure would help to identify content which teachers themselves considered necessary for all students to learn. By way of augmentation, systematic review was made of the general literature in the subject area. The review covered items most frequently mentioned in course bibliographies as well as the more recently published theoretical material (since 1950) in the fields of sociology, social psychology, social anthropology, social economics, social administration, political science, history, law and social philosophy and ethics.

To identify in all this material the major patterns of ideas relevant to a social work curriculum, specific content items were noted on separate slips and then sorted into increasingly more general categories as suggested by their points of similarity. In this way concepts and categories evolved inductively at various levels of abstraction.

In the fall of 1957 the project director attempted to test reactions to these tentatively emerging formulations of desirable content for the social services curriculum. Visits were made to a number of

---

of this project with another one also under this writer's direction, the public social services project. It also seemed a desirable contribution from a semantic standpoint. The term "social services" appeared to be used in the literature with meanings which at one extreme confused it with casework service programs and at the other seemed to signify the whole range of community services. But the advisory panel later thought the appropriate name for this content area should be "Social Welfare Policy and Services" (see page 38).

selected schools for discussions with deans, curriculum committees and selected faculty.[3] These visits also provided helpful insights into and understanding of (1) the reasons why present objectives were being used, (2) the problems being encountered in attaining present objectives, and (3) the ideas being entertained for changing objectives.

It had been planned to obtain, through questionnaires, ratings of the validity, importance and usefulness of the various content items from certain groups of persons including students, graduates, faculty, practitioners and subject matter experts, but time did not permit doing this. Consequently, chief reliance for evaluative judgments was placed upon the advisory panel to the project. The sixteen educators and practitioners who composed the panel met three times with the project director, each meeting lasting two days. Working as a whole group and in committees, the panel members contributed invaluably in such ways as helping to clarify problems and to identify issues, advising on priorities in staff work, proposing suggestions, making critical evaluations of staff memoranda, agreeing or disagreeing with proposed formulations, and making definite recommendations.

Following the final panel meeting in December 1957, project efforts were concentrated upon improving the formulation of content aspects of objectives and upon formulating appropriate behaviors to be developed by students in relation to the specific content items. At this stage of work, the statements of objectives that emerged were "screened" for professional relevance and educational importance against the final revised statement on *The Nature of Social Work*, which had been designed to serve as a "philosophy screen" for all study projects.

The formulation of objectives for teaching in the social services area of the professional curriculum that is presented in this report benefited from preliminary discussions with other members of the Curriculum Study staff. Time did not permit, however, any systematic correlation of the various objectives developed by individual projects.

The writer desires to express appreciation and gratitude for the

3 Four schools were visited: Howard University, University of Michigan, University of Tennessee and the University of Toronto.

stimulation, guidance and assistance contributed to his work by the persons who served on the advisory panel and by his colleagues on the study staff.

The remainder of this report is divided into seven chapters. The chapter immediately following discusses present school curricula in the social services content area. Chapter III provides the framework used in this project for selecting desirable curriculum objectives. Chapter IV lists and discusses recommended curriculum objectives. Chapters V through VII discuss briefly the sets of objectives regarding problem, policy and provision. Illustrative learning experiences by which the recommended objectives may be attained and a brief summary constitute the concluding Chapter VIII.

CHAPTER II

The Present Curriculum on the Social Services

This chapter is prologue. It provides background information essential to understanding current problems in developing a professional curriculum on the social services. Current course offerings are held in profile against a backdrop of changing conceptions about a professional curriculum in this content area.

The background of the present curriculum on the social services appears to reach back to the beginnings of professional education. Courses with titles similar to those currently grouped by schools as belonging in "the social services" content area of the curriculum appeared in the earliest school catalogs. Indeed, so many courses appeared in these early catalogs as to cast some doubt upon the frequent assertion that the early schools of social work saw their purpose largely in terms of vocational training. For example, in examining the available catalogs at the Council on Social Work Education for eight of the oldest schools of social work,[1] it was found that *more* courses of a social services character were offered by the schools in the past than in the present. One school offered directly, and in cooperation with other university departments, a total of 32 courses with social services content in 1925 but only 6 in 1957. Another school listed 22 such courses in 1930 and 10 in 1957. A third listed 9 in 1934 and 5 in 1957.

Furthermore, early courses *more often* than recent ones tended to emphasize broad social, cultural, economic and political perspectives on professional problems. This is indicated by the offerings of one school in 1919 under such course titles as Evolution of Modern Industry, Social Economics, Social Ethics, and Social Treatment of Poverty. This particular school now offers only courses with such program-focused titles as The Social Services, Public Welfare, Family and Child Welfare, and Medical and Health Services. At another school, courses offered in 1927 were

---

[1] Catalogs for one school date back to 1919, for three to the early 20's and for four to the early 30's.

entitled Development of Social Institutions, Character of Racial Groups, Industry I, II, III, Professional Review of the Social Sciences, Objectives and Perspectives in Social Work, Elements of Law for Social Workers and Social Legislation. Today this school offers a limited number of courses with titles suggestive of a focus on selected programs, the general history and philosophy of social work, and Professional Problems.

CONCEPTIONS OF THE CONTENT AREA

If not so numerous nor so broadly gauged as courses of old, are current course offerings more appropriate to professional education? Are schools agreed on the courses that should be required of all students? Do these required courses cover the same basic content? Do they constitute a unified and cohesive part of the total professional curriculum?

These are questions that have been among the central concerns that brought schools of social work together in the Association of Schools of Social Work in 1919. Indeed, from its very inception the Association attempted to tackle them. A formal curriculum committee was not appointed, however, until 1930–31. The charge to this first curriculum committee has remained the basic charge of subsequent curriculum committees: "to find some body of knowledge which may be called basic and which should be given by all schools engaged in training for social work." Review of the work of the various curriculum committees, as recorded in minutes and other documents in the files of the Council on Social Work Education, reveals that they generally subscribed to the idea that some "social services" content should be part of the requirements set for "minimum preparation for a person to be considered a professional social worker."

Conceptions of what this content should be seem to have undergone three significant changes of orientation. In the earliest view, this content was thought of as separate subjects organized as *single courses,* such as those listed above. A new view evolved in a curriculum committee working under the chairmanship of Charlotte Towle from 1941 to 1944.

Finding the subject-centered concept of curriculum content too inflexible for readily assimilating new knowledge or for reflecting changing needs in practice, this committee suggested an organization of content around "basic fields of knowledge," each including a series of related courses. The committee identified *eight basic knowledge fields* as relevant to professional education for social work. One was designated Public Welfare.[2] Public Welfare was defined comprehensively to include social, political, economic, and scientific factors and forces in "all forms of public assistance as well as governmental responsibility for the care and protection of children, for the sick, the mentally ill and defective and for legal offenders." Illustrative materials were developed by special committees to promote coverage of basic content by all schools. One such document, for example, outlined the content of a basic course in public welfare and listed titles for other courses that might be given as part of a public welfare sequence. Another document illustrated how schools might develop objectives appropriate for student learning of public welfare content.

The high hope that the "basic eight" concept would result in a cohesive curriculum providing fundamental content for social workers failed to materialize. Many schools interpreted the concept narrowly as prescribing a minimum number of courses required for Association membership. They simply established a required or elective course in each field, often giving these courses the names of the particular knowledge fields covered. Typically, school catalogs began to list Public Welfare as the title of the school's only required course in this knowledge field.

A curriculum committee appointed in 1951 decided to abandon the basic eight concept as "outmoded and unrepresentative of current thinking." It favorably received a suggestion from the then executive secretary of the Association, that four broad *areas of content* be established as the framework for schematizing the professional curriculum. Two *areas of content*—described as centering on "knowledge of society and its institutions" and "knowledge of the structure of the social services"—were eventually integrated by

2 The other seven basic fields: social casework, social group work, community organization, social administration, social research, medical information, and psychiatric information.

the committee to form a single content area designated in the official *Curriculum Policy Statement* of 1952 as "the Social Services" and defined and described as follows:

> The social work curriculum should provide . . . knowledge and understanding of the social services, their development, and their relation to the social order, to social change, and to community needs . . . knowledge and understanding of the social services should be acquired through study of current social welfare programs under public and private auspices, together with their historical development and progress toward meeting the needs of people. Such an approach implies study of the social services as they are affected by social, political and economic influences; evaluation of the social services in relation to the social and individual needs which they are designed to meet; appreciation of the contribution of its leaders; and an appraisal of the role of the social work profession in the formulation and execution of progressive social policy. Attention should be given to the range, variety, and interrelationships of social welfare programs and their actual implementation in the light of accepted standards.

Adoption of this curriculum statement, close upon publication of the Hollis-Taylor report on social work education,[3] caused many schools to examine their curriculum anew. In February 1955 a Curriculum Study committee of the Council, with the Reverend Felix Biestek as chairman, canvassed the schools by questionnaire for reports on progress made to date in curriculum revision. A list of courses then offered in each content area was requested with specific information about the title of the course, whether or not required of all students, class hours allotted to it, and its place in the sequence of courses.

Fifty schools responded. A brief summarized report on findings was published in a special curriculum issue of *Social Work Education* for October 1955. Since this report described only the courses required of casework students, this writer reexamined the original questionnaire returns to obtain a more comprehensive picture of what schools were offering as social services courses and what

---

[3] Ernest V. Hollis and Alice L. Taylor, *Social Work Education in the United States* (New York: Columbia University Press, 1951).

changes had been introduced in this content area of the curriculum since 1952. Concurrently, school catalogs, course outlines and other available curriculum materials were studied for supplementary information, particularly in regard to the content of courses required of all students. Major findings are briefed below.

CHARACTERISTICS OF CURRENT COURSE OFFERINGS

Three facts stood out from this analysis.

First of these facts was that not many schools were using the curriculum-area concept as a basis for classifying their course offerings.

Although all the schools answering the questionnaire attempted in their replies to group their courses into the three areas outlined by the *Curriculum Policy Statement,* only 19 did so in official catalogs of courses. Of this group of 19, only 11 schools used The Social Services as the heading of one of the three groupings of courses.[4]

The second fact highlighted by the analysis was that the term "The Social Services" was not used consistently by the schools as the term of reference for courses listed under this heading.

This was often apparent from the course titles themselves. Only infrequently did titles contain the words "social services." By far the most common term of reference was "social welfare." Other titles carried such terms as "welfare" or "social work." Whatever distinctions these varying terms were supposed to imply were not made clear by the actual course content, as indicated by course outlines. For example, practically the same content appeared to be covered by a course entitled Philanthropy and Social Welfare as by one entitled The History of Social Work or The History of the Social Services.

[4] Headings substituted for The Social Services were Organization and Administration of the Social Services, Organization and Administration of Welfare Services, Administration and Organization of Social Welfare Services, Social Welfare Organization, Basic Social Welfare Courses, Public Welfare Administration, Social Work Organization and Problems, and Social and Cultural Factors.

The confusion of these terms is perhaps inevitable in view of the fact pointed out by the United Nations survey that "In no country has terminology been so standardized as to make possible the assignment of precise meaning to such terms as 'social welfare,' 'social service,' 'social work' and 'welfare work.' " [5] A number of studies have attempted differentiating definitions, but, as Friedlander has noted wryly, "It has been difficult, however, to reach an agreement which is universally accepted." [6]

Harry M. Cassidy, who probably did more than anyone else to spread the use of the term "the social services" in the United States and Canada, has defined it as follows: "The social services in the modern community may be defined as those socially provided services that are concerned primarily and directly with the conservation, the protection and the improvement of human resources." [7] In England, where the term originated, its meaning traditionally encompassed, in Lord Beveridge's phrase, all the programs directed toward combatting the "Five Giants" in the path of social progress —Want, Disease, Ignorance, Squalor and Idleness. Richard M. Titmuss recently reported that the term is being applied in Great Britain today "to more and more areas of collective provision for certain 'needs.' It has indeed acquired a more elastic quality; its expanding frontiers, formerly enclosing little besides poor relief, sanitation and public nuisances, now embrace a multitude of heterogeneous activities." [8]

In two recent writings the term is given institutional definition. According to Witmer and Kotinsky, "The social services constitute that social institution [which arises] to provide remedies where individuals in any society find the basic social arrangements for meeting human needs are not available or do not work." [9] A somewhat similar notion of the term is expressed by an English writer:

[5] United Nations, Department of Social Affairs. *Training for Social Work—An International Survey* (New York: Columbia University Press, 1950), 5–6.
[6] Walter A. Friedlander, *Introduction to Social Welfare* (New York: Prentice-Hall, 1955), 3.
[7] Harry M. Cassidy, *The Terminology of Social Work* (Toronto: University of Toronto, 1948), 2. Mimeographed.
[8] Richard M. Titmuss, "Social Policy and Social Work Education," paper given at the Arden House Conference on Social Policy in Social Work Education, April 22–25, 1957, 22–23.
[9] Helen L. Witmer and Ruth Kotinsky, eds., *Personality in the Making* (New York: Harper and Brothers, 1952).

"The social services constitute one of the groups of social institutions which society has developed to meet the personal needs of its members, needs which are not adequately or most effectively met by other means either by the individual from his own or his family's resources or by commercial or industrial concerns." [10]

The term "social welfare" will be defined in the next chapter as the key term of reference for the curriculum area now referred to as "the social services." [11] However, its confusion with the term "welfare" may be noted at this point. In current usage the term "welfare" appears to have two references. It may mean either the same thing as social welfare, being but a shortened expression of this term, or it may have a more general meaning than intended by the term social welfare. In the latter sense it may be a synonym for the term "general welfare," as employed in the Preamble of the Consitution of the United States. Thus used, it signifies a range of values, interests and activities extending to protection against enemies from within and without; maintenance of law and order; development and maintenance of facilities for communication and transportation; promotion and regulation of commerce and industry; sanitation and health; conservation of natural and human resources; physical, economic and social planning; and so forth.

The third important fact emphasized by the analysis was that content about "the structure of the social services" heavily outbalanced content about "society and its institutions."

Practically two-thirds of the schools reporting in the 1955 survey required all students to take only courses focused on program aspects. Thirteen of the fifty reporting schools required students to take only one course of this character and twenty-nine required them to take two courses. A small scatter of schools required students to take more than two program-focused courses; five required that three such courses be taken and two required four such courses. One school had no course requirement of this character. Some of the schools which had a requirement of only one or two

10 Joan Eyden, "Social Services in the Modern State," *Case Conference* (February 1955), 19.
11 See page 28.

program-focused courses also required students to take courses in related subject areas. Thus, eight schools had a course requirement in law, five in philosophy, eleven in history, seven in cultural-social factors and seven in policy issues and problems. Six schools listed their first administration course and four their first community organization course as part of the requirements in the social services area rather than in the social work methods area. A number of schools appeared to have difficulty deciding how to classify courses in these subjects by content area for the 1955 survey. Some took refuge in an "other areas" category which the survey questionnaire thoughtfully provided. Under this "other areas" heading were listed courses required in law, administration and community organization (by one school each), cultural-social factors (by four schools), philosophy and ethics (by six schools) and "seminars on social work" and "seminars on social welfare" (by a total of ten schools).

Findings in regard to these aspects of the 1955 survey may be briefed as follows:

The courses covered varying types and numbers of programs.

All required program-focused courses dealt with combinations of programs rather than single programs. The rationale for program selection was rarely made explicit in course outlines. Programs which originated in or were stimulated by the depression of the '30's, particularly income-maintenance programs, were the most universally covered. At some schools child welfare and health and medical care programs received separate course treatment. But the more common practice appeared to be to group these programs in a single course together with additional programs, varying in number. Represented in some combinations were programs in correction, rehabilitation, mental health, housing, services to veterans and services to specific age groups. Most commonly omitted programs were those in the fields of group work and recreation, community organization and international social welfare. Programs under private auspices received comparatively superficial treatment compared to public programs. (Only one school reported a full course on Private Welfare Services.)

Similarly titled courses often had different content.

Course outlines of similarly titled required courses often showed widely different content. For example, some courses entitled Public Welfare dealt only with current selected problems in the administration of public welfare services. Other courses so entitled focused on history, most often American history. Still other courses with the title Public Welfare emphasized legislative and organizational aspects. Although the insurance and public assistance programs were generally covered by public welfare courses, there was considerable variation as to inclusion of other public programs in these courses.

Topics covered varied widely.

Examination of course outlines revealed varying combinations and amounts of materials on the following topics:

Underlying concepts of social welfare, and definition of terms;
Environmental background, including existing and potential reality factors in the determination and operation of social welfare programs;
Human needs and problems dealt with by social agencies;
Legal rights and responsibilities defining and governing social welfare activities;
Social policy problems and issues;
Historical development of social welfare programs, with some consideration of the contribution of leaders;
Professional philosophy and organization of the social work profession;
The range, variety and interrelationship of social welfare programs;
Organization, administration and community relations of social agencies;
Research for guidance and validation of social welfare programs.

By far the bulk of content related to the item on the range, variety and interrelationship of social welfare programs.

The professional point of view was not often made explicit.

Course outlines reflected a generalized treatment of content without much pointing up of professional areas of responsibility and operation in terms of professional values, goals, functions or methods. Broad citizen interests were emphasized. Technical operations and problems were commonly discussed in general terms rather than in terms defining the services social welfare programs require specifically from the profession of social work.

Historical rather than current or future issues received emphasis.

Considerably more content was included on the problems and issues that confronted social work in the past than on those facing it today and in the future. For example, the income-maintenance programs were rather generally treated in terms of the historic factors in their rise, with little attention given to forces affecting their development today or in the future.

The treatment of content was more often in single units not treated comparatively, and in terms descriptive rather than analytical, factual rather than conceptual.

The course outlines of required courses show little use of comparative, analytical or conceptual methods of treatment. Highly condensed outlines of individual programs tend to be organized around such facts about program as objectives, establishment, coverage and eligibility, benefits or services, and administrative structure and financing. That the emphasis was factual is attested by the minutiae about programs included in course outlines.

The courses in the content area lacked integration.

A number of schools had arranged all the courses offered in the social services content area in a numbered series under a general title, such as Social Welfare I, II, III. Despite this arrangement, the courses grouped together often represented compartmentalized content either by program, such as income-maintenance and "social services" or by aspects, such as legal, historical, and philosophical.

Course organization varied greatly.

The 1955 questionnaire survey had two distinctions. It supplied the only relatively comprehensive information on how schools classify their courses by content area, and it constituted the only source available for comparative study of the required or elective status of course offerings, since school catalogs often neglect to furnish specific information of this character.

Facts about course organization revealed in the 1955 survey may be summarized as follows:

1. *Number of courses:* A total of 355 courses were classified by the schools as belonging in the social services content area. The large number of courses per school suggested much fragmentation of content. The number of courses per school ranged from two to twenty-two and the median number of courses was eight.

2. *Kinds of courses:* Courses focused on public welfare programs predominated. A fairly large number of schools, but less than half of the total, offered special courses on child welfare and health and medical care. Small numbers of schools offered courses on other programs. History, philosophy and ethics, law, and policy issue courses were offered by a fourth to a half of the schools.

3. *Requirement status of courses:* Fewer than half the courses offered, or 165, were required of all students by the schools offering them. The distribution of courses between required and elective varied greatly among schools. Less than half the schools which offered history, philosophy or law courses required that all students take them. Of schools offering courses on rehabilitation, housing, school social work, and international social welfare, none listed these courses as required for all students, although specific groups of students were required to take selected numbers of them (*e.g.,* medical social work students were required to take the rehabilitation course where it was offered). Twelve schools offered no elective courses in the social services area. The number of required courses per school ranged from one (at six schools) to six (at one school operating on a quarter system). The largest group (at seventeen schools) had a three-course requirement in this content area.

4. *Sequence of courses:* Nearly two-thirds of the schools indicated a social services course requirement of at least one course in the second year of the Master's program. The placement of particular courses in the first and second years was not uniform except for courses on policy issues, which were placed in the second year by all schools offering them. Slightly more schools placed their

course offerings in law, history and philosophy in the first year rather than in the second.

5. *Classroom hours devoted to courses:* Most schools allotted between 75 and 199 classroom hours to required courses in the social services area. This is a smaller number of hours, on the average, than was required by courses in the human growth and behavior content area or in the social work methods area. Only 7 schools devoted less, and 5 more, than the range of 75 to 199 hours to courses in the social services area. Classroom sessions typically extended to two hours a week per semester or three hours a week per quarter.

6. *Course credits:* In general, a student was permitted to accumulate 8 credits in the social services content area toward the customary 60 credits required for completion of the master's program. (Only 36 of the total credits can be acquired in classroom work. The remainder must be earned in field work and research). A number of courses with similar titles and descriptions carried different credits at different schools.

7. *Course revisions:* With "integration" of content an avowed objective, many schools made extensive changes in social services courses after 1952 to bring them into closer conformity with the Council's *Curriculum Policy Statement.* Between 1952 and 1955 ten schools had re-structured all or substantially all their courses in this content area. In addition, twenty-seven schools had either: added or dropped single courses; added or revised content of existing courses; combined or shifted one or more courses from elective to required status; changed the name of courses; shifted the sequence of courses; added or decreased class time; increased or decreased course credits.

Between 1955 and 1957, some seventeen schools made changes in their catalog listing of courses in this content area. The changes involved more adding of new courses than dropping of old ones. This was contrary to the trend toward fewer courses indicated by the revisions made in the 1952–1955 period. Most of the new courses related to rehabilitation, corrections, child welfare and public welfare.

8. *Methods of course instruction:* Most of the schools had course outlines for most of the courses offered in the social services area.

These outlines often listed many subdivisions of topics covered. Their format and style lacked uniformity even within the same school. A number of course outlines lised the content for each class session. Many had attachments of required or suggested reading lists. These bibliographies were often very extensive and quite similar. Syllabi had been developed for only a few courses. Assignments to students varied considerably in number and type.

The most common assignment consisted of a short paper and a longer term paper. The choice of subject was often left to the student completely or within the limits of offered choices. Midterm and final examinations were not scheduled at most schools; the term paper seemed to be the major examining device. Classroom instruction was primarily by a combination lecture-discussion method. A small number of courses were handled as seminars. Only occasional mention was made of the use of visual and audio aids, observational visits or guest speakers. Some courses involved the student in planned individual and group project assignments requiring reports to the class in the form of talks, panel and round table discussions, socio-dramatic presentations, and so on. With few exceptions, teaching assignments in this content area were limited to one or two full-time faculty members. Part-time faculty often taught the law course and occasionally the courses on child welfare, health and medical care, and community organization. Most of the full-time faculty teaching in the social services area also taught in other content areas. At most schools the dean or director taught one or more courses in the social services content area.

9. *Formulation of course objectives:* Objectives are, in the dictionary sense of the word, the ends toward which action is desired. In educational circles the term signifies the directions set to guide learning and teaching activity. A more specific meaning of the term is provided by Dr. Ralph W. Tyler. "Objectives," he says, "indicate the kinds of changes in the student to be brought about so the instructional activities can be planned and developed in a way likely to attain these objectives; that is, to bring about these changes in students." [12] This definition is the one to which the whole Curriculum Study is oriented. Essentially it involves, as

[12] Ralph W. Tyler, *Basic Principles of Curriculum and Instruction* (Chicago: University of Chicago Press, 1950), 29.

Dr. Tyler informs us, the task of delineating "the kinds of behavior to be developed in the student and the content or area of life in which this behavior is to operate." [13] (By behavior Tyler means the knowledge, the skills and the ways of thinking that the student is expected to acquire; by content, the concepts, the facts, the principles, the issues to which the behavior applies.)

School curriculum materials furnished few statements of objectives that satisfy this definition. A small number of schools have statements which list the general objectives of all courses in the social services content area. These statements are often only paraphrases of the description of the social services area contained in the Council's *Curriculum Policy Statement*. Most of the individual course outlines simply list topical headings of content covered. As Dr. Tyler has observed, objectives stated in the form of topical headings "do indicate the areas of content to be dealt with by the students but they are not satisfactory objectives since they do not specify what the students are expected to do with these elements." [14]

A large number of course outlines included a brief introductory paragraph ostensibly intended to generalize the objectives of the course. Sometimes these statements were worded in ways that emphasize what the instructor intended to do in the course. For example: "to acquaint the student with existing resources"; "to impart the rudiments of social welfare organization"; "to provide knowledge of the judicial process"; "to convey knowledge about the development of social work." Dr. Tyler characterizes objectives stated in this form as unsatisfactory on at least two grounds. First, they are not really educational objectives because the real purpose of education is not to have the instructor perform certain activities but to bring about significant changes in the student's behavior patterns. And, secondly, they fail to provide the criteria against which the student's learning can be evaluated.

Another group of course outlines stated objectives in terms of descriptions of the plan of organization or procedures of the course. One example: "The purpose of the course is to describe and evaluate the methods by which society provides for the protection

13 *Ibid.*, 30.
14 *Ibid.*, 29.

and welfare of socially disadvantaged children." Another: "The objectives of the course are to examine as a matter of information the state-federal legislative and administrative provisions for the mentally ill and to consider certain modalities of social work participation in psychiatric organization and services." In the Tyler view, objectives stated in this form obviously tell what the students and teacher are to do together in the classroom but lack clear focus upon the changes desired in student behavior. Furthermore, they are too general to suggest the kinds of learning experiences and teaching procedures by which student changes are to be achieved.

Problems of vagueness and generality are also raised by such recurring phrases in statements of objectives as: "to prepare the student to act responsibly as a social worker in regard to proposals and programs designed to meet social needs"; "to stimulate the student to critical thinking about social work responsibility"; to increase the student's identification with the profession"; "to confirm the student's convictions that each member of the profession holds responsibility for promoting social change"; "to enable the student to make contributions to the development of social policy." From the Tyler standpoint, phrases like these need further clarification in the direction of specifying the behavior which can be taught and learned in the specific content areas covered by the courses.

SUMMARY

This analysis of the present curriculum in the social services content area suggests that it lacks cohesiveness and focus upon basic professional content. The specific content covered by currently required courses is often diffuse rather than concentrated, fragmentary rather than integrated, factual rather than conceptual, descriptive rather than analytical. Course organization and instruction vary considerably. Course objectives are most commonly stated in terms of topical headings to be covered or the teachers' planned activities or class procedures. Few statements of objectives were found which focus on the student as learner and specify what behavior he is expected to develop in what content areas.

These findings suggest as focal points for improving the existing curriculum the following questions, now largely unresolved:

1. What content would provide a balanced and cohesive description of the subject area?
2. What concepts would bring the content into an appropriate professional and graduate educational focus?
3. What behavior should the student be expected to develop in learning this content?
4. What would be the best way of stating as curriculum objectives the content and behavior expectations from students?

These unresolved questions will be dealt with in the next two chapters.

CHAPTER III

A Framework for Selecting Desirable Objectives

When a curriculum content area appears to lack cohesiveness in basic content, it may be because it lacks what is termed in the social sciences a common "frame of reference." The importance of a common frame of reference is suggested by Julian Huxley's observation anent the state of contemporary knowledge: "The lack of a common frame of reference, the absence of any unifying set of concepts and principles, is now, if not the world's major disease, at least its most serious symptom." [1]

This chapter attempts to formulate a common frame of reference to guide the selection and formulation of desirable objectives for the curriculum content area under study. We conceive the overall function of a frame of reference to be threefold: to identify and draw the boundaries of a content area, to define and describe systematically the important elements within it, and to provide analyzing and ordering tools for fitting pieces of content together so that each may relate to the other as coherent parts of a recognizable whole. The frame of reference proposed here is intended to provide a guide to help schools realize their long sought goal of a cohesive, basic professional curriculum.

UNDERLYING ASSUMPTIONS

Before we proceed to define the several components of this frame of reference, its underlying assumptions will be stated briefly so as to make clear the premises on which it rests:

1. By virtue of its nature as a "social" profession, social work carries a responsibility to help guide the society of which it is a part to make desirable and necessary decisions and provisions for

[1] Julian Huxley, *New Bottles for New Wine: Ideology and Scientific Knowledge* (London: Royal Anthropological Institution of Great Britain and Ireland, 1950).

enhancing the social functioning of its members in their individual and group life.

2. When we speak of a *profession* doing something we are referring not to an abstraction but to the persons who make up the professional group. Individually and collectively these persons carry an obligation to assume and perform professional roles in society. It follows that professional education must center upon the student as a future member of the profession so as to equip him to fulfill the profession's responsibility to society.

3. If the profession's social responsibility is to be discharged effectively, each member will have to acquire not only relevant knowledge but the will and the ways—the conviction, commitment, competence and what Agnes Meyer calls "social diplomacy" [2]—to apply that knowledge effectively.

4. As to the knowledge necessary for this purpose, the professional person needs, not knowledge that is specific only to the concrete and the immediate, but knowledge that is sufficiently generalized and systematized to have wide and varied application.

5. Finally, the professional person is a product of cumulative education. By the time he enters the graduate phase of professional education he should have acquired the necessary broad academic foundations for enlarging, deepening, and using knowledge in professional practice.

COMPONENTS OF THE FRAMEWORK

Out of these considerations have evolved the six components of the frame of reference, discussed in the pages that follow. They comprise interlocking hypotheses which have been established in part inductively and in part deductively. Their purposes are to provide (1) a rationale for developing curriculum objectives; (2) an orienting social work educational philosophy; (3) a focusing viewpoint; (4) an anchoring term of reference; (5) a unifying set of concepts; and (6) a challenging approach. The first two components were available to the project as parts of the plan for the total Curriculum Study.

2 Agnes E. Meyer, "No Man Is an Island," *Social Work*, I (July 1956), 3.

The rationale and procedures which guided this project as well as the entire Curriculum Study in identifying and formulating desirable curriculum objectives have been formulated by Ralph W. Tyler in his *Basic Principles of Curriculum and Instruction*. In the Tyler approach to curriculum development, objectives comprise a set of statements of the purpose of a plan of instruction. Each objective specifies the kinds of behaviors students are expected to develop within certain content areas. The desirability of a particular objective is determined by its relative importance, consistency and compatibility with a formulated educational philosophy.

THE ORIENTING EDUCATIONAL PHILOSOPHY

This component is formulated in a statement, *The Nature of Social Work,* prepared by Werner W. Boehm, director of the Curriculum Study, which served as the "screening instrument" for all projects to select the most desirable objectives among many identified. This statement conceives of social work education as oriented to a constellation of certain defined values, goals, functions, and activities which are believed by the Curriculum Study staff to constitute the nature of the profession.

THE FOCUSING VIEWPOINT

This, and the next component on term of reference, evolved from recognition that the objectives of a professional curriculum must focus upon and be limited to content that has professional relevance and significance.

Identification of professionally relevant and significant content from the vast body of knowledge about society which falls within this curriculum area may be approached from a number of standpoints, such as:

1. A behavioral viewpoint, to perceive the significance of personality in social organization;
2. A philosophical viewpoint, to illuminate man's tendency to systematize his ideas and idealize his systems of social thought and action;

3. An historical viewpoint, to provide perspective for understanding social change in the context of changing times and
conditions;

4. An institutional viewpoint, to give insight into the nature of
society and the processes by which the social order achieves
orderliness and stability of response to life's persistent challenges.

Obviously a combination is necessary for broad understanding
in any knowledge area, since all aspects of knowledge are inti-
mately conjoined and mutually influential. For purposes of systematic analysis, however, it would seem desirable to bring one
aspect of knowledge into primary focus.

The one aspect of knowledge about society deemed in this project to be especially relevant to the profession of social work is that
concerned with society's institution-building for orderly meeting
of human needs. An institutional emphasis draws attention to the
social functions and structures of society and their planned crea-
tion, change and coordination. One of the earliest definitions of
this institutional characteristic of society, and still among the most
useful, is that of William G. Sumner: "An institution consists of
a concept (an idea, notion, doctrine, interest) and a structure. The
structure is a framework, or apparatus, or perhaps only a number
of functionaries, set to cooperate in prescribed ways at a certain
conjuncture. The structure holds the concept and furnishes the
instrumentalities for bringing it into the world of facts and action
in a way to serve the interests of man and society." [3]

The more recent sociological literature identifies six elements
of a social institution: a fairly stabilized form of behavior (behavioral element) of human beings grouped together (organizational element) for a common purpose (conceptual element) sanctioned and regulated by society (normative element) and made
operative through materials, tools and equipment (physical element); integratively, these elements form a distinctive culture (cultural element).[4]

[3] William G. Sumner, *Folkways* (New York: Ginn and Company, 1907), 53–54.
[4] Particularly helpful in clarifying the function and structure of social institutions
were the following sources: Stuart F. Chapin, *Contemporary American Institutions*
(New York: Harper and Brothers, 1935); James K. Feibelman, *The Institutions of Society* (London: George Allen and Unwin, 1956); Joyce O. Hertzler, *Social Institutions*

Generally speaking, social institutions perform for the whole society the following important functions:

conservation, by assuring continuity of the social heritage;
socialization, by supplying the settled modes of behavior and the relatively fixed forms of social evaluation to on-coming generations;
cooperation, by creating the social machinery through which individuals carry on their differentiated but interdependent activities; and
control, by canalizing conduct, inhibiting behavior believed prejudicial to the general welfare or interests, and assuring behavior which experience has indicated to be desirable.

Social institutions take several forms:

as *social structures (e.g.,* family, state, church, etc.)
as *social attitudes, customs or beliefs (e.g.,* child-centeredness, democracy, natural law, etc.)
as *social roles (e.g.,* father, bureaucrat, priest, etc.)
as *social practices (e.g.,* foster care, taxation, worship, etc.)

The process of institutionalization is relative to many factors in the environment. In less developed societies social institutions arise gradually without deliberate planning (crescive process) and tend to become traditionalized. Modern societies, grown complex and impersonal, tend to proliferate an ever-widening range of social institutions primarily in a deliberate or planful way (enactment process). Each social institution in a particular society has a relative critical and strategical position; for example, in most societies, including our own, the family is recognized as the most important and essential of all social institutions. On the other hand, institu-

---

(Lincoln: University of Nebraska Press, 1946); Marion J. Levy, Jr., *The Structure of Society* (Princeton: Princeton University Press, 1952); Robert M. MacIver, *Community: A Sociological Study* (New York: The Macmillan Company, 1924); and Florian Znaniecki, "Social Organization and Institutions" in *Twentieth Century Sociology,* edited by Gurvitch and Moore (New York: The Philosophical Library, 1945). Helen L. Witmer pioneered in analyzing social work from the standpoint of the concept of social institution, in *Social Work: An Analysis of a Social Institution* (New York: Farrar and Rinehart, 1942).

tions like state, church and property have not universally been held in equally high esteem.

From the standpoint of an institutional approach, this curriculum area emphasizes content on the functional-structural-change aspects of society. Behavioral, philosophical and historical content should be included wherever it contributes to understanding institutional aspects of society.

THE ANCHORING TERM OF REFERENCE

The suggestion of an institutional focus is not intended to imply that all social institutions come within the scope of this curriculum area. Clearly, so broad a focus would not be appropriate for a professional curriculum. The principle of professional relevance demands a narrowing of focus upon those institutional aspects of social life which express society's concern for the well-being of its members as individuals and in family and community groups. We propose the term "social welfare" to describe this limitation of focus. As noted in the preceding chapter, this term is already used by many schools to designate the curriculum content area as a whole or the majority of the courses into which the content is organized.

It is recognized that there is no general agreement on the meaning of this term. The confusion of definitions available in the literature suggests that social workers, as Znaniecki says of sociologists, "have not yet generally and fully accepted the professional standards of symbolic communication which are recognized as binding in older and more stabilized sciences." [5]

Part of the problem of definition is that the scope and nature of social welfare institutional development varies considerably among countries and communities, since they necessarily reflect stages of social and economic organization attained.[6] Moreover, the dimensions of the term are continually being extended by such factors as technological developments, discoveries of causes of human dysfunction, and increasing recognition that social welfare institutions are needed to advance "a social order in which all persons

[5] Znaniecki, *op. cit.*, 172.
[6] Donald S. Howard, "Social Welfare," *Encyclopedia Americana*, Vol. 25, 1957. See also United Nations, Department of Social Affairs, *Methods of Social Welfare Administration* (New York: Columbia University Press, 1955), 282–285.

have opportunity to find fulfillment of their nature and destiny both as individuals and as groups in interdependence." [7]

As Wilensky and Lebeaux point out,[8] two major streams of philosophy flow into current conceptions of social welfare. In the light of a philosophy of individualism social welfare is conceived primarily as a mechanism of need fulfillment brought into play when the family and the economic system do not function adequately or when the individual, because of old age or illness or the like, cannot make use of them. From this point of departure social welfare institutions have the function of "residual agencies,"—taking care of emergencies and withdrawing when the regular social structure (the family and the economic system) is again working properly. Seen in this residual, temporary, substitute character social welfare services often carry the stigma of "dole" and "charity." On the other hand, from the standpoint of a philosophy of social responsibility, the term tends to be defined as a "proper, legitimate function of modern industrial society in helping individuals achieve self-fulfillment. The complexity of modern life is recognized. The inability of the individual to provide fully for himself, or to meet all his needs in family and work settings, is considered a 'normal' condition." [9]

We propose that the term *social welfare* should be used as the anchoring term of reference in selecting objectives for this curriculum. For such use, we define the term broadly to denote a related system of social institutions in a society, which are unified by common values, goals and operational principles. The social welfare institutions share values rooted in conviction about individual worth and dignity and social interedependence and responsibility. Their goals lay common stress upon the importance of social services to the growth, development and enrichment of human beings for more effective social functioning. Their basic operational principles are suggested by the following definition in a United Nations document, which is described as a modification, by substitut-

---

[7] *Churches and Social Welfare*, Vol. III: *The Emerging Perspective: Response and Prospect*, ed. E. Theodore Bachmann (New York: National Council of the Churches of Christ in the U. S. A., 1956), 101.
[8] Harold L. Wilensky and Charles N. Lebeaux, *Industrial Society and Social Welfare* (New York: Russell Sage Foundation, 1958), 139.
[9] *Ibid.*, 140.

ing italicized words, of the definition of health developed by the World Health Organization:

Social Welfare is a state of complete physical, mental and social well-being and not merely the amelioration of *specific ills*. The enjoyment of the highest attainable *standard of life* is one of the fundamental rights of every human being without distinction of race, religion, political belief, economic or social conditions. The *welfare* of all peoples is fundamental to the attainment of peace and security and is dependent upon the fullest cooperation of individuals and States. The achievement of any State in the promotion and protection of *social welfare* is of value to all. Unequal development in different countries in the promotion of *social welfare, particularly in relation to the abolition of poverty,* is a common danger. *Normal* development of the child is of basic importance; the ability to live harmoniously in a changing total environment is essential to such development. The extension to all peoples of the benefits of *social, psychological, medical and related knowledge is essential to the fullest attainment of the social welfare.* Informed opinion and active cooperation on the part of the public are of the utmost importance in the improvement of the *welfare* of the people. Governments have a responsibility for the *social welfare* of their people which can be fulfilled only by the provision of adequate social and economic measures.[10]

THE UNIFYING SET OF CONCEPTS

In developing this fifth component of the framework for selecting desirable curriculum objectives, the characteristics of social welfare knowledge posed a major problem, to wit:

1. It is highly changeable. The rapid changes and developments in social welfare produce such an endlessly changing stream of information as to cause one teacher to complain that "laboriously acquired knowledge of the details of each program is frequently rendered obsolete by legislative and administrative changes almost before the academic year is over." [11]

2. Its complexity aggravates the problem of changeability. At

[10] United Nations, Department of Social Affairs. *Training for Social Work—An International Survey* (New York: Columbia University Press, 1950), 6–7.
[11] Eveline M. Burns, *Social Security and Public Policy* (New York: McGraw-Hill Book Company, 1956), x.

the present time materials from sociology, social anthropology, social psychology, social economics, political science, social administration, law, and other disciplines are all included to some extent. More complex material of this character is in the offing in view of a renewed interest of schools in the assimilation and use of knowledge from the social sciences.[12]

3. It is highly qualitative. Many of the basic questions in social welfare cannot be answered by objective data or scientific inquiry alone. They are oriented to perspectives and convictions derived from social philosophy, ethics, religion, and history. As Porter R. Lee has said, "Much of what we do in social work we do because, on the whole, we prefer a civilization in which such things are done to one in which they are not." [13]

4. And its sheer magnitude! Obviously what there is to know has long passed the point of exceeding the possibilities of any one curriculum, any one teacher, or any one student. Today more than ever selection and synthesis are necessary requisites of effective education.

How can such vast, varied and voluminous material be reduced to fundamentals for professional education? On the basis of the content analysis and consultation described in Chapter II, a set of concepts has been identified which we propose should be used to organize the content of this curriculum area.[14] The concepts are stated at a high level of abstraction to permit encompassing as many lower level abstractions and empirical details as meet the test of professional relevance.

The first three concepts are intended to describe or characterize core knowledge about social welfare to be covered in this curriculum area. These concepts are termed "problem," "policy" and "provision" and are defined below. The other four concepts establish major variables in light of which the core concepts require analysis. These concepts, also defined below, are termed "rights,"

12 Katherine A. Kendall, "Education for Social Work" in *Social Work Year Book, 1957* (New York: National Association of Social Workers, 1957).
13 Porter R. Lee, *Social Work: Cause and Function and Other Papers* (New York: Columbia University Press, 1937), 19–20.
14 As used here, the term concept means "an abstract idea that refers either to a class of phenomena or to certain aspects or characteristics that a range of phenomena have in common." Social Science Research Council, *The Social Sciences in Historical Study.* Council Bulletin, 64: 91. 1954.

"responsibility," "capability," and "role." While it is intended that these seven concepts might be given central place in the social welfare curriculum, the teaching of other concepts is not precluded. Among such additional concepts are those taught in the undergraduate phase of professional education and in other areas of the graduate curriculum which, it is assumed, would be reintroduced for their reference value and for reinforcement of learning.

Core Knowledge Concepts

1. *Problem.* A proper use of this concept requires that it be clearly distinguished from the term "need" with which it is often confused. In the dictionary sense, a need is a normal state of excitation to which all living things are subject. Its nature is inferred from the behavior of the person. It may or may not become manifest as a problem. Whether it does will depend upon whether and to what extent it cannot be satisfied or met. When this happens the need arouses in the person experiencing it, or reactively in others, some "perplexity or distress" which in turn poses a "quandary or difficulty or conflict for which solution, settlement or handling may be felt necessary." [15] Even at that point the problem may or may not be a social problem. It is not a social problem if, presumptively or as a matter of fact, it can be worked out with available resources institutionalized in society. It is a social problem if this is not the case and if this fact poses a threat to some value or functional requirement of society.

It is in this latter sense that the term *problem* is proposed as one of the three major concepts of content in this curriculum area; that is to say, because it brings under scrutiny society's institutional provisions for meeting needs. Other connotations of the term as it is used here refer to such component elements of a problem as its focus, range, cause and effect, form of manifestation, and challenge and opportunity.

2. *Policy.* As used here, the term *policy* is intended to refer to the process of social decision-making by which a course of social action is determined, formulated and promoted (policy-making),

[15] *Webster's International Dictionary.*

as well as to the product of that process (the resulting policy). The concept has several dimensions related to the kinds of policy for which the profession has concern: social policy, social welfare policy, public policy, and social work policy. In its most popular context, as social policy, two meanings of the term will need explication to students. A British writer has defined its earliest meaning to represent a movement toward mitigating the effects of industrialism, as a

> quest for freedom for men, women, and children, whose lives were becoming hasty, brutish and short because they were being reduced to the function, as Samuel Butler put it, of domestic animals attendant upon machines.[16]

The same writer defines a more current meaning of the term as a movement to establish "civic minima."

> But what modern social policy has done is not merely to attack industrial evils: It has made also the positive declaration of civic minima. These minima have become social imperatives—imperatives that condition the lives of infants and the aged, of adolescents and adults.[17]

For study purposes in this curriculum area the term is intended to convey also the need for analyzing the relation between assertions and reality in the formulation of policy solutions; for uncovering errors of logic in policy diagnosis; for projecting both the short run and the long run consequences of policy proposals; and for appraising not only the substantive values (such as work, health, security) but also the procedural values (such as public works, compulsory health insurance, protected retirement) [18] embodied in policy. Other elements of the term that require analysis are its source in social trends, its evolutionary and planned development, its values and ends-means bases, its issues, and its strategy.

3. *Provision.* As used here, the term *provision* connotes the popular idea of making things available that are needed or desired.

---

[16] Hugh L. Beales, *The Making of Social Policy,* L. T. Hobhouse Memorial Trust Lecture (Oxford: The Clarendon Press, 1946), 10.
[17] *Ibid.,* 7–8.
[18] Lester G. Seligman, "The 'Public Policy' Orientation and the Social Science Course," *Journal of General Education* (January 1955).

More technically, the term is intended to connote ways of meeting social welfare problems or of implementing social welfare policy. It may take the form of programs, services, agencies and personnel. As components of the concept *provision,* each of these forms must be viewed in its historical, philosophical, legal, and community contexts.

Analytical Concepts

The next four concepts are intended to serve as analytical tools to enhance understanding of the three core knowledge concepts. These anaytical concepts epitomize much content now included in this curriculum area but handled as merely descriptive background information. We propose that the concepts should be translated into searching questions such as: What *ought* to be done? What *should* be done? What *must* be done? What *can* be done?

4. *Rights.* This concept is part of a duality because rights and responsibility can be viewed as the two sides of a coin. A right *to receive* becomes somebody's responsibility *to do.* The concept puts the question, What *ought* to be done? into the consideration of *problem, policy* and *provision.* It has assumed increasing importance in urbanized, impersonalized societies. Underlying it is the assumption that men are related responsibly in contractual association with one another, based on mutual respect and consideration which may often require legal definition.

In the study of the core knowledge concepts, the concept *rights* raises questions around such values as social justice, equity, protection against arbitrary action. Significant points of reference arise from the *right* to receive consideration of one's problems, opportunities, service requirements, and needs for privacy and personal choice. The concept is useful also to identify and analyze conflicts among rights, and between rights and correlative obligations, as well as trends toward expansion or limitation of rights to social welfare services.

5. *Responsibility.* In looking at the corollary of *rights,* expressed in the question, What *should* be done? moral and ethical action is emphasized. The term encompasses a cluster of concepts which

make important distinctions among the kinds of responsibility for social welfare borne by the individual, the family, and such institutions or associations as industrial, governmental, sectarian, philanthropic, and civic. The concept also connotes the responsibility of citizens, individually and in groups, for participating in the policy-making and support of social welfare services; the responsibility of the profession for defining service goals, ensuring quality of service; and the responsibility of administrative agencies for economic and efficient provision of service—in other words for accountability and stewardship in the conduct of social welfare enterprises.

6. *Capability.* This concept asks of *problem, policy* and *provision* the question, What *can* be done? It assumes that the world in which social work operates is a multi-dimensional and dynamic environment—geographic, physical, cultural, technological, and human—whose resources must be continually searched out and assessed for possible use in the service of mankind.

7. *Role.* This concept poses the question, What *must* be done by *whom?* It is a term that has assumed a major position in recent sociological and social psychological theory to link theories of personality with theories of small groups. A standard definition does not yet exist but fairly common usage attributes two meanings to it: first, as designating the parts one performs in group life and second, as describing expectations about how certain parts shall be performed regardless of who the performer is. The term assumes that a person has to perform many different parts or roles in life. Because these roles are reciprocal (*e.g.,* parent-child, worker-client) they often determine the nature of social interaction. The concept suggests many significant points of inquiry and issues in the study of social welfare *problem, policy* and *provision.* It may be used to identify roles that must be performed for maintaining and building social groups, as well as for carrying out the essential group tasks. Another possible use of the concept would be to clarify the requirements of effective performance in various social welfare roles such as client, practitioner, technician or expert, clerk, and citizen.

THE CHALLENGING APPROACH

We come now to the sixth and last component of the frame of reference for selecting desirable objectives. In its development a major emphasis of the Hollis-Taylor report was kept in mind, which called for the preparation of social workers for responsibilities of "statesmanship and leadership." [19] These are qualities few possess, but professional education can make a positive contribution to the development of at least one of their major ingredients —intelligence as harnessed by appropriate professional values in the service of professional goals. In suggesting a conceptual organization of curriculum content, the strategy is to place emphasis upon a conceptual type of learning to equip the student with *keys* to knowledge rather than minutiae of knowledge. This kind of learning trains the mind as it stocks it. It challenges the student to an active, critical and inquisitive search for knowledge that is professionally relevant and significant. As a memorandum of a committee on university education for the professions at Columbia University points out:

> The power to continue and enlarge one's education is of the greatest importance now that current knowledge in the sciences and the professions is constantly being outmoded by new knowledge. Knowledge is expanding so rapidly that it is impossible to give a man all the knowledge he will need, and the effort to do so merely by adding new courses is certain to fail. The expansion of knowledge will continue, and the student must be prepared in intellectual power as well as in attitude to acquire and utilize the new knowledge for himself . . . Indeed, knowledge acquired by the student through his own efforts is more truly his than information received from the instructor, put down in his notebook, and then given up at examination time.[20]

The memorandum puts the issue in a larger perspective by adding:

> The contrast is . . . between intellectual discipline and information; between accuracy of comprehension and precision of expression, and

19 Hollis and Taylor, *op. cit.*, 141–45, 150–52.
20 Columbia University, University Council, *Report of Columbia University Committee on University Education for the Professions* (New York: Columbia University Council, April 4, 1955). Mimeographed.

vagueness and generality in both comprehension and expression; between thoroughness in dealing with a few subjects and superficiality in covering many subjects; between courses dealing critically with general principles and courses giving specialized information; between the forming of the mind and the imparting of information; between dealing with the student as a producer and treating him as a consumer.[21]

The kind of challenging approach proposed here is an accepted emphasis of education at a graduate level. It is especially important in the content area we are concerned with, which the student often approaches with a rather considerable stock of miscellaneous information—much of it misinformation, unthinking opinion and downright prejudice—which he will not attempt to change with as much interest and motivation as he brings to relearning in the curriculum areas concerned with human behavior and social work methods. More often than not his attitude toward learning social welfare content is characterized by deep skepticism as to its professional relevance.

The kind of conceptual learning suggested here should make intellectual demands upon the student by confronting him with the challenge of the content, both quickening and deepening his understanding of the problems it poses, the policy decisions it demands, and the provisions that it requires.

SUMMARY

This chapter has outlined the frame of reference that guided the selection of the objectives for the social welfare curriculum area that are set forth in the next chapter. Desirable objectives were defined as statements of the behaviors expected to result from student learning in specified content areas. The relevance and significance of identified objectives for professional practice constituted the primary selection criterion. Other criteria included a focusing viewpoint, an anchoring term of reference, a unifying set of concepts, and a challenging approach.

[21] *Ibid.*

CHAPTER IV

Recommended Objectives
for Teaching Social Welfare Policy
and Services: An Overview

This chapter lists recommended educational objectives for the curriculum area under study. These are the objectives which were found to meet best the tests of desirability described in the preceding chapter. Emphasized are the major concepts under the three core content areas—*problem, policy* and *provision*—to be learned at the master's level of social work education.

RECOMMENDED CHANGE OF TITLE
FOR CONTENT AREA

As the heading of this chapter indicates, a new name for this content area is also proposed. This new title, "Social Welfare Policy and Services," is thought to have the following advantages over the present one, "The Social Services":

It describes more fully and accurately the appropriate scope and nature of content to be covered.
"Social Welfare," as the anchor term of the title, suggests the broad institutional scope of content appropriate for presentation. The terms "policy" and "services" suggest the aspects of social welfare whose relation could be explored most meaningfully at the graduate level of professional education.

It describes more clearly the appropriate graduate treatment of content covered.
As was noted in Chapter II, the title "The Social Services" seemed to have encouraged fragmentation of content at factual and descriptive levels. The new title serves to bring into focus major

factors in the field of social welfare. Also it suggests a problem-solving approach to teaching the content.

THE NATURE AND PURPOSE OF THE RECOMMENDED OBJECTIVES

It will be recalled that in the Tyler definition, objectives state the educational purposes which a school seeks to attain. They "become the criteria by which materials are selected, content is outlined, instructional procedures are developed and tests and examinations are prepared." [1] They are most useful for these purposes if expressed "in terms which identify both the kind of behavior to be developed in the student and the content or area of life in which this behavior is to operate." [2]

On the grounds that it is difficult for an instructor to keep clearly in mind too many differentiations in behavior and content, Tyler suggests that a list containing somewhere between seven to fifteen behavioral categories and between ten and thirty content categories is likely to be found more satisfactory than a larger or smaller number. However, this degree of condensation poses the problem of obtaining an appropriate level of generality or specificity. He advises that "Other things being equal more general objectives are desirable than less general objectives." [3]

Tyler recommends fewer behavioral than content categories because many differentiations in behavior are hard to make, but content can be differentiated almost endlessly. A desirable degree of content differentiation should extend, in his view, at least to the point of indicating "areas of content that are important and appropriate and . . . to put together areas that are reasonably homogeneous areas for sampling content specifics . . ." [4]

Caution is necessary in order that "Each of the terms used in the behavioral headings and in the content headings should have meaning, so that they do not represent vague generalities which have no concrete significance to the curriculum maker and thus

[1] Tyler, *op. cit.*, 3.
[2] *Ibid.*, 30.
[3] *Ibid.*, 37–38.
[4] *Ibid.*, 38.

cannot guide him in the next steps of curriculum development." [5]

Following these injuctions, the recommended objectives formulate seven behavioral categories, and a total of twenty content categories divided among the three major content areas of *problem, policy* and *provision*. In view of this high condensation, the exposition that follows in this and the next three chapters makes some attempt to clarify, define and describe each objective that is stated. A parenthetical word of caution is necessary. The formulated objectives are intended to guide the development, not of a *single* course, but of a *series* of sequential course offerings which all students in the Master's program are required to take to fulfill degree requirements.

DEFINITION OF BEHAVIOR CATEGORIES

Seven categories of behavior are utilized to describe the behavior aspects of the objectives, the specific ways of knowing, doing and feeling that students should develop as they learn certain content. These particular behavior categories are not ideal, but they provide some differentiation of the behavior desired, and are at the same time few enough to be easily remembered in planning instruction.

"KNOWING" BEHAVIORS

Two types of knowing behavior should be developed in the student:

1. a *knowledge* of the salient characteristics of content and of the dependable sources where specific information may be obtained, and

2. an *understanding* of the meaning and relationship of the important facts, principles, concepts, and issues that describe a body of content.

"DOING" BEHAVIORS

Two types of behavior are to be sought in this category:

3. *assessment skill* in appraising the validity and reliability of knowledge and drawing logical inferences and conclusions, and

[5] *Ibid.,* 38.

4. *interpretation skill* in expressing the sense and significance of knowledge clearly and persuasively in written and oral ways.

"FEELING" BEHAVIORS

Three types of behavior should be aimed at in this category:

5. a *scientific viewpoint* toward knowledge and its use, necessary for perceiving the difference between fact and opinion and for reaching logical and reasonable judgments;

6. a *social viewpoint* toward knowledge and its use, necessary for recognizing and identifying with the humanitarian considerations in life or content areas; and

7. a *professional viewpoint* toward knowledge and its use, necessary for recognizing and identifying with professional value, goal and role considerations in life or content areas.

For the sake of simplifying the use of the behavior designations it is suggested that they be viewed as continuous rather than discrete items in an ascending order within each of the three behavior areas. Thus only one behavior term need be used to specify the full dimensions of the behavior area, knowing, doing or feeling. When the term understanding is used, it should be construed to include the behavior of knowledge; when interpretation skill is used, it should be construed to include assessment skill; and when social viewpoint is used, it should be construed to include a scientific viewpoint, while the use of professional viewpoint should be construed to include both the scientific and the social viewpoints.

This specification of the kinds and dimensions of behavior changes to be sought immediately suggests that the study task of the student of social welfare policy and services includes much more than merely acquiring information: it requires a breadth and depth of learning that will enable the student to gain increased knowledge of general content and sources which furnish specific information; deeper understanding of important facts and generalizations; increased skill in making assessments and interpretations; and firmer orientation to scientific, social and professional outlooks that characterize social work's view of human problems, the policies they call for, and the provisions they require.

A tabular view follows of recommended objectives for teaching "social welfare policy and services" in both behavioral and content

Tabular View of Recommended Objectives for Teaching "Social Welfare Policy and Services"

CONTENT AREAS IN WHICH BEHAVIORS ARE TO BE DEVELOPED BY THE STUDENT	Knowledge	Understanding	Assessment skill	Interpretation skill	Scientific viewpoint	Social viewpoint	Professional viewpoint
A. PROBLEM							
1. as manifest need	x	x			x		
2. as person-centered	x	x					x
3. as universal yet singular	x	x			x		
4. as cause and consequence	x	x			x		
5. as institutional lack or dysfunction	x		x				x
6. as challenge and opportunity	x	x					x
7. as requiring a service solution	x	x				x	
8. as requiring social work help	x		x				x
B. POLICY							
9. as social commitment	x		x				x
10. as social movement	x		x				x
11. as planned social change	x	x					x
12. as manifesting the desirable	x		x				x
13. as manifesting the possible	x	x					x
14. as posing social issues	x		x				x
15. as social action	x		x				x
C. PROVISION							
16. as mobilized resources of society	x	x					x
17. as organized in a social agency	x	x					x
18. as client-centered service	x	x					x
19. as teamwork	x		x				x
20. as geared to serving the total community	x	x					x

specification. In the next three chapters some exposition will be attempted of the conceptual components of the statements of objectives outlined above. Limitations of time make possible only a sketch development of the core ideas, and this *suggestive* character of the discussion should be kept in mind.

CHAPTER V

Recommended Curriculum Objectives in Regard to Social Welfare Problem

The discussion in Chapter III of the term *problem* bears repetition at this point.

A proper use of this concept requires that it be clearly distinguished from the term "need" with which it is often confused. In the dictionary sense, a need is a normal state of excitation to which all living things are subject. Its nature is inferred from the behavior of the person. It may or may not become manifest as a problem. Whether it does will depend upon whether and to what extent it cannot be satisfied or met. When this happens the need arouses in the person experiencing it, or reactively in others, some "perplexity or distress" which in turn poses a "quandary or difficulty or conflict for which solution, settlement or handling may be felt necessary." Even at that point the problem may or may not be a social problem. It is not a social problem if, presumptively or as a matter of fact, it can be worked out with available resources institutionalized in society. It is a social problem if this is not the case and if this fact poses a threat to some value or functional requirement of society.

It is in this latter sense that the term *problem* is proposed as one of the three major concepts of content in this curriculum area; that is to say, because it brings under scrutiny society's institutional provisions for meeting needs. Other connotations of the term as it is used here refer to such component elements of a problem as its focus, range, cause and effect, form of manifestation, and challenge and opportunity.

Problem phenomena do not now receive systematic attention in the curriculum. Some attention is given to them in the methods courses but primarily from a clinical point of view. Social welfare courses often provide broad descriptions of problems in presenting material on the programs of service established to deal with them. Conceptual treatment of problem phenomena is, however, rarely attempted.

The conceptual approach to teaching problem phenomena is here directed toward eight objectives, appropriate to a problem-solving profession. The assumption is made that, for the social worker to engage effectively in problem-solving, he must learn the characteristics of the problems which confront social work. This need is viewed here as requiring concentrated learning around the following interrelated conceptions of *problem:*

1. *Problem* manifests human need.
2. *Problem* is person-centered.
3. *Problem* is universal yet singular.
4. *Problem* has causation and consequences.
5. *Problem* is a condition of institutional lack or dysfunction.
6. *Problem* presents challenge and opportunity.
7. *Problem* calls for solution in the form of social welfare service.
8. *Problem* calls for professional social work help.

These core ideas are embodied in the following eight curriculum objectives that relate to *problem.*

Objective I:

$$\left.\begin{array}{c}\text{UNDERSTANDING,}\\ \text{ASSESSING, AND}\\ \text{VIEWING SCIENTIFICALLY}\end{array}\right\} \text{PROBLEM} \left\{\begin{array}{l}\text{AS}\\ \text{MANIFEST}\\ \text{NEED}\end{array}\right.$$

This objective is intended to add clarity to the conception of problem by distinguishing the often confused terms "problem" and "need," so that the student may view and assess more scientifically the phenomena subsumed under each term. The conception of *problem as manifest need* implies that problem must not be thought of as identical with need. Problem is not the equivalent, or interchangeable, term for need that it is so often made out to be in the literature; distinctions exist that are important for the student to grasp. For example, problem is concrete in character and can be observed and assessed from the evidence of the difficulty that an individual, group, or other social unit is having in its functioning. On the other hand, need is inferential rather than obvious in nature; its character is delineated on the basis of some hypothesis formulated on the evidence of the very behavior it is intended to explain.[1]

Need is frequently assumed to underlie a problem as a sort of "first cause," imputedly being either something desired or valued, or something felt to be lacking for fulfillment or satisfaction.[2]

Since need arises in an individual organism, it is essentially an individual attribute which cannot be ascribed to social unts, or to such aggregates as groups and communties, without implying their existence as human organisms. (This is the implication of such expressions as "community needs"; Charlotte Towle points a way to avoiding this fallacy by referring to needs which many people have as "common human needs.")[3]

The pitfalls of using one form of the term need, *unmet needs*, require stress in view of the great popularity of this phrase in social work. Martin Wolins's discussion of the distinction between *unmet needs* and *problem* has special pertinence in this connection:

> Traditionally, those needs which are not met in the customary, routine, socially accepted and acceptable manner have been called "unmet needs." The term "unmet needs" conveys the impression that the need which has not been met can be satisfied in the standard manner as though the failure to meet it has not occurred. This is often untrue. Why was the need an unmet need in the first place? Apparently something went wrong in the relationship between the person and the social institutions which until this time satisfied each other. We may speak of this something which goes wrong as a lack of equilibrium, a certain loss of reciprocal functioning . . . [between] man and the institution which has ordinarily met his present need . . . To emphasize the difference between needs which are routinely met and those which are not met for whatever reason and thereby require additional, often therapeutic, services, the latter will be called problems and not "unmet needs."[4]

[1] C. Addison Hickman and Manford H. Kuhn, *Individuals, Groups and Economic Behavior* (New York: The Dryden Press, 1956), 208.
[2] Dorothy D. Lee, "Are Basic Needs Ultimate?" in *Personality in Nature, Society and Culture*, eds. Clyde Kluckhohn and Henry A. Murray, 2nd ed. (New York: Alfred A. Knopf, 1953), 338–9.
[3] Charlotte Towle, *Common Human Needs* (New York: American Association of Social Workers, 1952).
[4] Martin Wolins, *Social Welfare Problems and Services in Berkeley, California* (Berkeley: University of California School of Social Welfare, November 1954).

As a problem-solving profession, social work's primary concern presumably is with problem and not need. Its primary responsibility is not itself to meet need but to see that need is met by institutions in society regularly constituted for the purpose, or to help create such institutions. Social work intervention in the needs-meeting situation is appropriate whenever need is not met and *problem* results.

Objective II:

$$\left.\begin{array}{l}\text{UNDERSTANDING,} \\ \text{ASSESSING, AND} \\ \text{VIEWING PROFESSIONALLY}\end{array}\right\} \text{PROBLEM} \left\{\begin{array}{l}\text{AS} \\ \text{PERSON-} \\ \text{CENTERED}\end{array}\right.$$

This objective is aimed at making explicit the profession's conviction that it is the human being who must be the central concern and the primary test of professional service. It implies the importance, in teaching as well as in practice, of a focus upon the person-with-the-problem rather than upon the problem abstracted from the person—even while, as a matter of analytical convenience, emphasis is placed upon the broad dimensions of a problem as manifested in the life of the group, community and society of which the person is a part.

The objective suggests the need to select and organize such teaching content about problem as will provide the student with basic knowledge for understanding and making proper assessment of the relation of *problem:*

1. to the whole person's needs and goals;
2. to the person's various biological, psychological, social and spiritual needs and goals;
3. to the person's changing needs and goals at various stages and ages in his growth and change; and
4. to the requirements and goals of the various social systems of which the person is a member, especially the family, community and nation.

Some of the focal questions that require exploration in identifying, defining and assessing problem areas of concern to the profession of social work are these: Who and how many people have the problem? How much general awareness is there of it and who considers it a problem? What is known about the problem? What does it mean to those who have it and to others in the immediate circle of family, community and society? What are the historic and prevalent attitudes, opinions and ideas about the problem, and in what ways and to what extent has social responsibility for doing something about it been recognized and accepted? How has the willingness to deal with it been influenced by such forces as cultural expectations (*e.g.,* the American ideal of self-sufficiency); changing institutional functions (*e.g.,* lessened economic role of the family); changing structures of society (*e.g.,* urbanization); and changing social roles (*e.g.,* role of housewife)? Who have been the leaders and what has been the history of movements for awakening society to responsibility for dealing with the problem?

Several negative as well as positive implications are intended by the objective. It is hoped, for one thing, that it would discourage a symptom-focused teaching approach, in view of the fact noted by Kahn that "This step from symptom-focused to person-focused is a major one and has not yet been achieved in handling broad areas of social pathology." [5]

It is further hoped that the objective would discourage a partializing of people in analyzing the problems they present. As the studies of Community Research Associates attest, a critical need of social workers is to be able to see all problems as interconnected, and people and their problems as constituting a wholeness.[6]

Objective III:

$$\left. \begin{matrix} \text{KNOWING,} \\ \text{ASSESSING, AND} \\ \text{VIEWING SCIENTIFICALLY} \end{matrix} \right\} \text{PROBLEM} \left\{ \begin{matrix} \text{AS UNIVERSAL} \\ \text{YET} \\ \text{SINGULAR} \end{matrix} \right.$$

This objective alludes to the truism that "everybody has problems but no two people have exactly the same problem." The objective suggests the importance of familiarizing the student with such characteristics of problems as their universality, magnitude, variety, and changeability in statistical as well as clinical terms.[7]

[5] Trude W. Lash and Alfred Kahn (eds.), *Children Absent from School* (New York: Citizens Committee on Children, 1949), 22.
[6] Bradley Buell *et al., Community Planning for Human Services* (New York: Columbia University Press, 1952).
[7] Paul E. Meehl, *Clinical Versus Statistical Prediction* (Minneapolis: University of Minnesota Press, 1954).

In the course of studying curricular materials many diverse classification systems were found to be used for grouping problems by their common characteristics. There were no indications that the rationale and limitations of particular classification systems were explicit parts of student learning. That they should be so presented would seem desirable if uncritical learning is to be avoided and the student helped to appreciate that problems are not molecular units but configurations, and yet that no hypothesized set of problem categories can altogether encompass their variations.

Not only should the student learn the rationale and limitations of classification systems for analyzing problems, but he should also be impressed with the importance of using accurately whatever classification system he may adopt for purposes of problem analysis. This point is exemplified by the finding that, while curricular materials abounded with references to Charlotte Towle's formulation of common human needs, their specifications of it were often at variance with the original list.

Objective IV:

$$\left.\begin{array}{c}\text{UNDERSTANDING,}\\ \text{ASSESSING, AND}\\ \text{VIEWING SCIENTIFICALLY}\end{array}\right\}\text{PROBLEM}\left\{\begin{array}{l}\text{AS CAUSE}\\ \text{AND}\\ \text{CONSEQUENCE}\end{array}\right.$$

It is all too easy for the student to fall into the habit of labeling everything and anything that may seem to be connected with a problem as "cause" or "consequence" or both, unless definite precautionary steps are taken by the teacher. This objective aims to alert the student to critical thinking about causation. He needs to learn to examine problem phenomena for possible causative factors in at least the spirit of Northrop's injunction that "none of the social sciences has laws of a causal type, like those of physics, enabling one to deduce the state of a social system tomorrow from its state today. Nevertheless, this is what one must have before there are scientific grounds for asserting that social events are caused by any previous specified events." [8]

8 F. S. C. Northrop, "Ideological Man in His Relationship to Scientifically Known Natural Man," in *Ideological Differences and World Order*, ed. F. S. C. Northrop (New Haven: Yale University Press, 1949), 409.

The difficulty of establishing scientific causal laws in social welfare problem areas has not discouraged efforts at causative explanation. The literature reveals a tendency to explain problem phenomena in one of three major ways: (1) picturing causation in terms of a single factor, such as poverty, personality, class and caste stratification, and so forth; (2) picturing causation in terms of a community configuration of factors; or (3) picturing causation in terms of other multiple causation theory, in which are combined various social, economic, political, and geographical conditions and forces thought to be operating in cultural contexts.[9] The student should become critically familiar with these systematic explanatory approaches, to counterbalance any possible tendency on his part to lump together an indiscriminate and often interminable list of so-called "factors" and "variables." He also needs to gain perspective on the swing in preoccupation with certain causation theories, especially the shifting emphasis between explanations centered in environmental and personality factors.

Objective V:

UNDERSTANDING,			AS INSTITUTIONAL
INTERPRETING, AND	}	PROBLEM {	LACK OR
VIEWING PROFESSIONALLY			DYSFUNCTION

This objective emphasizes social work's concern about the functioning of society as a whole as well as of its individual members. The concept of *problem* as a condition of lack or dysfunction in society's institutions for meeting needs has central importance for understanding that social welfare institutions and social work have functions beyond therapeutic services; they extend to services aimed at changing, creating and coordinating society's whole structure. The concept requires the student to understand that human problems, diverse as they appear in their outward forms, manifest gaps or inadequacies or inefficiencies of the needs-meeting institutions of society.[10] In light of this, the problems of society in fulfilling its responsibility for the well-being of its members need to

9 Richard C. Fuller, "Sociological Theory and Social Problems" in *Analyzing Social Problems*, ed. John Eric Nordskog *et al.* (New York: The Dryden Press, 1950), 21–22.
10 Lawrence K. Frank, *Society as the Patient: Essays on Culture and Personality* (New Brunswick: Rutgers University Press, 1948), 1–20.

be understood as well as the problems that individuals and groups experience by reason of lack or dysfunction in society's institutional provision.

The student needs to learn what are the "functional requisites" of a modern society and what specific functional problems exist in such concerns of social life as the physical maintenance of the population; differentiation and assignment of social roles; communication; education; regulation of choice of goals and of means for attaining them; regulation of affective expression; socialization; control of disruptive forms of behavior; and institutionalization of desired behavior.[11]

The student should learn to identify and view the problems arising in these functional areas of society in a problem-solving context by determining: (1) the situations in which the problems appear, (2) the values believed threatened, and (3) the kind of outside action or help called for, particularly if, and what kind of, social work would be appropriate.[12]

Objective VI:

$$\left.\begin{array}{l} \text{UNDERSTANDING,} \\ \text{ASSESSING, AND} \\ \text{VIEWING PROFESSIONALLY} \end{array}\right\} \text{PROBLEM} \left\{\begin{array}{l} \text{AS} \\ \text{CHALLENGE AND} \\ \text{OPPORTUNITY} \end{array}\right.$$

One concept which this objective emphasizes is suggested by the observation of Foote and Cottrell that "The problematical situation is one where it appears that something can be done, something which is defined by the comparison of a better future and a worse present. Thus the concept of problems is closely linked historically and culturally with the idea of progress and the increase of man's power over nature." [13]

Besides suggesting the importance of viewing problem as amenable to progressive solution, the objective implies fundamentally the importance of what Lippitt and his associates call "an image of fluidity," and define as follows:

11 Levy, *op. cit.*, Ch. 3.
12 Francis E. Merrill, "The Study of Social Problems" in *Analyzing Social Problems,* ed. John Eric Nordskog *et al.* (New York: The Dryden Press, 1950).
13 Nelson N. Foote and Leonard S. Cottrell, Jr., *Identity and Interpersonal Competence: A New Direction in Family Research* (Chicago: University of Chicago Press, 1955), 177.

Nothing is static; improvement is always possible, provided, of course, we can agree on what really constitutes improvement. Consequently, we are always revising our definition of what is good performance, efficiency, effective use of our resources, etc. In itself, the idea that we can improve ourselves and our circumstances is a potent push toward innovation.[14]

Learning to view problems in the light of these concepts should stimulate the student to a recognition of the challenge that particular problems pose and the opportunities they afford for social solution. This kind of thinking is helped by acquaintance with criteria for assessing society's responsibility for problem-solving. Suggestive are the criteria proposed by Jessie Bernard, which she terms humanitarianism, dsyfunctionality, and utilitarianism and which may be defined by these questions: Does the problem cause actual pain or suffering? Does it threaten the functioning or survival of the group, community or society? Does it involve costs to the group, community or society? [15]

As Dr. Bernard points out, different answers have emerged at different times because of the different capabilities of society at the time. Thus a society in an age of economic abundance, such as ours, is capable of viewing pain and suffering broadly enough to meet not only problems of physical illness and hunger but also those of psychological anxiety and insecurity. A society at a poverty level is much less capable of this broad view of the problem.

Objective VII:

UNDERSTANDING,		AS REQUIRING
ASSESSING, AND	PROBLEM	A SERVICE
VIEWING SOCIALLY		SOLUTION

This objective is intended to stimulate thinking about *problem* in terms of the concrete solutions required from society, in the form of social welfare services and facilities. Several frameworks should prove helpful in seeing the implication of this objective. The student may be guided to discover, and to obtain factual de-

---

14 Ronald Lippitt *et al., The Dynamics of Planned Change* (New York: Harcourt, Brace & Co., 1958), 5.
15 Jessie S. Bernard, *Social Problems at Midcentury: Role, Status and Stress in a Context of Abundance* (New York: The Dryden Press, 1957), 104.

scriptions of, the programs, services and disciplines that have emerged in our society to deal with certain kinds of human problem. He may be encouraged to compare the functions and roles of the various disciplines involved in solving selected problems. Assessment may be required of the adequacy and effectiveness of programs and services available in a selected community to cope with certain problems.

Lists of problems published by national or local agencies [16] may be utilized to assess the availability of needed services. Cross-analysis of the problem lists of agencies in the same field of service helps to identify similarities or differences in philosophical, functional and structural approaches of agencies to problem-solving. Problem lists of the agencies of a community may also be studied to identify the nature of services offered in relation to problems of a physical, emotional, social, and spiritual nature, or in relation to problems that typically emerge at the various ages and stages of human life.

Objective VIII:

UNDERSTANDING,			AS REQUIRING
INTERPRETING, AND	}	PROBLEM {	SOCIAL WORK
VIEWING PROFESSIONALLY			HELP

To distinguish the problems or parts of problems for which society implicitly or explicitly holds the profession of social work responsibile to offer help, the Curriculum Study document *The Nature of Social Work* provides a suggested frame of reference. Social work responsibility for problem-solving is conceptualized in this document in terms of a set of interrelated values, goals, functions, and activities which are epitomized in this definition of the nature of social work:

> Social work seeks to enhance the social functioning of individuals, singly and in groups, by activities focused upon the social relationships which constitute the interaction between man and his environment . . . Social functioning . . . designates those activities considered essential for performance of the several roles which each individual, by virtue of his membership in social groups, is called upon to carry out. (Typically the individual has roles in social groups

[16] The list of client problems to be met by public welfare agencies appearing in the report on the public social services project may have interest in this connection.

related to such institutions as the family, the church, the school, work and leisure, and so on.)

In light of this proposition that the social worker's professional concern is with the enhancement of social functioning, what problems come within social work's competence? Systematic exploration of this question is the aim of this objective.

A point of departure for this type of exploration from the standpoint of social theory is suggested by Dr. Bernard's discussion of the relation between social problems and the social roles of members of a society characterized by abundance.[17] She advances a set of three role concepts for use in identifying the need for societal intervention in a human problem situation: role impairment, role confusion and role violation. These concepts lend themselves to adaptation for ascertaining the problems, or aspects of problems, for which social work intervention would be appropriate. The present writer offers here an adaptation to facilitate teaching of the objective under discussion.[18] It involves a rearrangement of the elements of Dr. Bernard's set of concepts, in which (1) her concept of role impairment is modified by including in its definition the idea of role violation, and (2) her concept of role confusion is modified by omitting one of its elements, "rolelessness," while the term "role deprivation" is coined to convey a more limited conception of Dr. Bernard's term "rolelessness."

It is proposed that the coined term, role deprivation, be given primary emphasis in exploring the nature of problems with which social workers have to deal. It directs attention to problems arising upon loss of a social role. Thus it involves understanding role deprivation due to change over which the individual often lacks effective control (e.g., loss of role of wife upon death of husband); dislocations in the economy (e.g., loss of role of family breadwinner with unemployment); cultural change (e.g., loss of role of independent farmer with urbanization of the population and trend toward large farm holdings); and so forth. The application of the concept of role deprivation to problem analysis should then identify for the student those problems which require social work

17 Bernard, op cit.
18 The casework project report offers another adaptation considered appropriate to identifying problems to be dealt with by the casework method.

services by reason of man's helplessness, anxiety and insecurity in a world of inexorable and rapid changes.

Problem analysis from the standpoint of role impairment and role confusion directs attention to role performance. The concept of role impairment should focus attention upon the inability of people to perform effectively the roles in which they are well established, because of limiting or handicapping conditions. Thus the use of this concept should highlight for the student problems ordinarily described as physical and mental illness, mental deficiency, disability and maladjustment arising from being in roles inappropriate to one's capacity, temperament, skill, or knowledge; or inappropriate by reason of being illegal or socially offensive, as the roles of prostitute, gambler, narcotics seller, burglar, beggar.

The problems that should come into the student's purview from attention to the factor of role confusion are of two kinds: (1) those where there is a lack of clarity about the nature of a role, with resultant confusion on the part of the people concerned as to what each is to expect from the other in their reciprocal roles (*e.g.*, parent-child, client-worker); and (2) those where there is a lack of compatibility or conflict among the various roles that a person is expected to perform. Lack of clarity about role expectations often arises when people move geographically or socially into new relationships and find in the new situation different perceptions of the role and expectations from it. Lack of clear role definition will also arise in situations where much latitude and improvisation is permitted in the way roles are to be performed. The incompatibility of roles is an increasing problem in a society like ours, characterized by much group life. Membership in many groups often places people in roles which conflict. Thus women become conflicted about their double roles as wives and workers; husbands become conflicted about the requirements of their home and fraternal roles; children become conflicted over loyalties to family and gang roles, and so on.

Problem viewed in the light of these role concepts should clarify for which problems society holds social work responsible to offer help to individuals, groups and communities. It should help the student to understand these problems in the light of factors strategic to their solution by social work service.

CHAPTER VI

Recommended Curriculum Objectives in Regard to Social Welfare Policy

Though more schools of social work offer content on policy now than in the past, an observation made by a workshop of the American Association of Schools of Social Work in 1952 appears still to be valid: "Social policy," the report stated, "is treated too frequently as peripheral to the main concern of education of the student for practice." [1] The objectives relating to this core concept are intended to rectify this situation. Through these objectives, *policy* content is given equal emphasis in the Master's curriculum with content on *problem* and *provision*.

The rationale for increased emphasis upon *policy* derives from the mission of professions in our culture to make their specialized knowledge and experience available for the benefit of the whole society; [2] and from professional conviction that the social worker has "by the nature of his work and his professional concern for people, a particular duty to perform in promoting and maintaining sound social policy." [3]

The objectives that follow were developed within the content of the definition of *policy* furnished in Chapter III, which describes the term as referring to

> . . . the process of social decision-making by which a course of social action is determined, formulated and promoted (policy-making), as well as to the product of that process (the resulting policy). The concept has several dimensions related to the kinds of policy for

[1] American Association of Schools of Social Work, *Toward an Integrated Program of Professional Education for Social Work*. Summary and Findings of Four Workshops. Annual Meeting, AASSW, 1952 (New York: Council on Social Work Education, 1952), 16.

[2] A. M. Carr-Saunders and P. A. Wilson, "Professions" in *Encyclopedia of the Social Sciences*, XII.

[3] American Association of Schools of Social Work, *Toward an Integrated Program of Professional Education for Social Work, op. cit.*, 17.

which the profession has concern: social policy, social welfare policy, public policy, and social work policy . . . Other elements of the term that require analysis are its source in social trends, its evolutionary and planned development, its value and ends-means bases, its issues, and its strategy.

Emphasized by the objectives are seven areas of learning about *policy:*

1. *Policy* represents social commitment.
2. *Policy* represents social movement.
3. *Policy* represents planned social change.
4. *Policy* manifests the desirable.
5. *Policy* manifests the possible.
6. *Policy* poses social issues.
7. *Policy* requires social action.

A brief description of these ideas follows.

Objective IX:

UNDERSTANDING,
INTERPRETING, AND   }POLICY{ AS
VIEWING PROFESSIONALLY   SOCIAL
                                 COMMITMENT

If anything can be said to distinguish the problem-solving efforts of a professional person, it is that he does not stop his work upon completion of direct service tasks; he takes responsibility to go beyond them, or sees to it that others do so, to translate the experience gained into improvements in the services themselves and the policies of the agency, community and nation that underlie them. An understanding of this feedback function of professional service is vital to an appropriate identification with the profession.

A professional service worker is committed to contribute to policy development in two basic professional roles: as member of the profession, and as representative of the profession. Membership in the profession involves assumption of commitments to client, employing agency, community and the larger society. To fulfill these commitments professionally, the student must try to become like and act like the ideal member image of the profession. He must accept as part of his personal motivation, and absorb as part of his personal functioning, the professional values, goals, functions, and concepts of acceptable professional behavior.

The necessity that a profession act in concert commits the members to joint planning and action on common professional concerns, and requires the student to become familiar with the history of the professional organization and its present characteristics as a corporate body. He should acquire current knowledge of the problems, positions, and activities of the professional organization and recognize that the strength, wisdom and effectiveness of professional activities depend essentially upon the active participation of individual members.

Basically needed are (1) conviction that the primary commitment of a social worker is to the social role of the profession; and (2) awareness of possible conflicts between that commitment and loyalties to employing agency or other organizations in which he has membership.

An important *policy* area that needs to be clarified is policy specific to agency function. The student should recognize that all agency personnel can contribute to policy-making from their job experiences. As Helen Perlman points out, agency policy can be strengthened by "the caseworker's perception and experience of client needs." [4] A major contribution by the executive to agency policy comes, in the words of A. Delafield Smith, when he recognizes that "It is not for the acting executive to *make* policy but to *derive* policy formulations from the operations of the professional disciplines within the agency." [5] For any social worker in any agency position to influence agency policy-making, he must have learned to understand existing policy—the direction it gives, the limits it sets, the resources it makes available, and the discretion it allows. He must have learned in addition the necessary skills (1) to interpret policy to those whom an agency serves and to those associated with serving the agency and (2) to assess agency policy in the context of the policy of other community service agencies. Most of all, he must have developed a sense of responsibility for reporting promptly when policy does not seem to fit, or to work in specific

[4] Helen H. Perlman, *Social Casework: A Problem-Solving Process* (Chicago: University of Chicago Press, 1957), 47.
[5] A. Delafield Smith, *The Right to Life* (Chapel Hill: University of North Carolina Press, 1957), 177.

situations, as well as appropriate techniques for marshalling relevant evidence and presenting it tactfully, persuasively and persistently.

The nature and demands of the social worker's role as representative of the profession constitute another focus in teaching *policy* as social commitment. The role of group representative is so typical in democratic societies as to have occasioned the definition of democracy as a process of multiplications of representatives. Typically, the role involves action by an individual over and beyond what he can do in private or general member capacity. Its core is power to act in behalf of the whole group, with the correlative obligation to wield that power in the group's interests. When acting as a representative of the profession, the professional person must act responsibly and accountably within the bounds of the power granted him. Learning to behave like an exemplary representative raises numerous educational questions because the ethics involved are as yet in a rudimentary state of distinction from the ethics governing private behavior. As one writer has observed:

> So far as a man is a representative, he is not himself. His scope and power of action may be enlarged, but his private discretion is reduced. He is not fulfilling his office, but either neglecting or exploiting it—both alternatives morally shocking—if in it he acts precisely the same as he does in his private relations.[6]

The ethics of acting as professional representative in policy matters should be explored with the student in light of both the opportunities it opens for greater service and the obligations it imposes for greater discipline in responsible and accountable behavior.

Objective X:

UNDERSTANDING, INTERPRETING, AND VIEWING PROFESSIONALLY } POLICY { AS SOCIAL MOVEMENT

The concept of *policy* as social movement emphasizes the importance of the social context within which policy is made and applied, since that context often explains why policy moves some-

---

[6] Thomas E. Jessop, *Social Ethics: Christian and Natural* (London: The Epworth Press, 1952), 48.

times forward and sometimes backward in pendulum swings, sometimes formally and sometimes spontaneously, sometimes abruptly and swiftly and sometimes slowly and gradually. The students should develop increased interest in reading the history of social welfare policy abundantly and with enjoyment, for better perspective on the causes espoused and the crusaders who ventured into battle for them.

Highly suggestive for teaching policy movements in historical perspective is the conceptual framework offered by Alva Myrdal,[7] who conceives social policy changes as going through three developmental stages. In the first stage policy is curative in intent. Private charity and public relief tend to be emphasized in measures such as caring for individuals or families who are poor, sick, disturbed, or otherwise in need of help from others. She characterizes this first stage as "paternalistic and conservative" in its underlying idea that cure of the worst ills is all the help needed.

The second stage becomes possible when curative bulwarks have been built. Society begins to recognize that it is not just the occasional individual and family who have need for outside help but considerable segments of the community. More universally applicable measures of help must, therefore, be provided. This is the period in which "insurance" measures are emphasized. A liberal philosophy is dominant which tends to conceive the pooling of common risks as enough of an answer to problems of unmet need.

The third stage emerges when the insurance period has achieved maturity and the field of social vision is cleared for a still more fundamental approach. This stage ushers in a social democratic era characterized by planning directed toward "prevention" of human ills. The scope of policy-making is thus widened to encompass solicitude for the total population and not just the indigent or the insecure. Says Mrs. Myrdal of this stage of policy development:

> This social policy will consist of cooperation in carrying through planned changes that are greater than the sphere of action of single individuals. It will be productive [adding] to the motives of charity and of justice, operating before . . . an economic interest . . . The costs of social reforms must cease to be regarded only as unproductive

[7] Alva Myrdal, *Nation and Family: The Swedish Experiment in Democratic Family and Population Policy* (New York: Harper and Brothers, 1941), 151–153.

expenses. They are the outlays for a productive social consumption which in time will raise the standards of the nation's effciency and earnings.[8]

In learning to understand *policy* as social movement, the student should at the same time become aware of the qualities which characterize the thinking of good historians. He should learn to see historical events in the flow of time, coming out of the past and into the future; to understand these events in relation to their contemporary social context, comprehending all aspects without subordinating any aspect; and to appraise the validity of the evidence of history, applying criteria of internal and external criticism.

Objective XI:

$$\left.\begin{array}{l}\text{UNDERSTANDING,}\\\text{ASSESSING, AND}\\\text{VIEWING PROFESSIONALLY}\end{array}\right\}\text{POLICY}\left\{\begin{array}{l}\text{AS}\\\text{PLANNED}\\\text{SOCIAL CHANGE}\end{array}\right.$$

An understanding of *policy* as planned change involves awareness that while change is the law of life, it can be either unplanned or planned. In our generation, the potentialities for "rendering change planful" [9] have grown enormously with our increasing control over time and space and nature. Today man can do more than merely react in responding to the need for change. He can act planfully. The student should learn to attune his professional attitudes to an activist point of view which recognizes that something has to be done about things that seem wrong and rejects the idea of passive resignation.

Policy-making must be viewed by the student as a process for "rendering change planful" by substituting action for drift and inertia, and purposeful, intelligent, appropriate action for blind, haphazard, routine reaction. Learning to recognize that policy-making is often irrational should not obscure the fact that the process is essentially orderly in nature. The orderliness of policy-making has been described by a number of writers. A useful

[8] *Ibid.*, 151. An application of this scheme to the analysis of the development of family-centered services will be found in Foote and Cottrell, *op. cit.*, Chapter 4.
[9] Foote and Cottrell, *op. cit.*, Chapter 5.

schematization for teaching this objective is the one offered by Chase E. Rothwell in a foreword to *The Policy Sciences*.[10] In his view, policy-making entails these steps: (1) clarification of goals; (2) exhaustive valuation of the situation to be met; (3) selection of a course of action by weighing the probable consequences of various alternatives; and (4) determination of optimum means for carrying out the action decided upon. The student should learn to assess policies in terms not only of process, but also of guiding professional principles.

Because public welfare legislation constitutes a major policy area, the student needs to learn to identify its distinctive features, and particularly the rationale of governmental intervention in the field of social welfare. He needs familiarity with the structures of governmental policy-making in social welfare and with the pressures brought to bear by outside influences such as political parties, special interest groups (including social welfare agencies and professional associations), and the executive department of government concerned.

Ability is needed to read policy statements intelligently and to distinguish permissive from mandatory language contained therein. Written policy is to be seen as an important lever for action against violations or inconsistent practices.

Objective XII:

UNDERSTANDING, INTERPRETING, AND VIEWING PROFESSIONALLY } POLICY { AS MANIFESTING THE DESIRABLE

Policy-making has been described as a process of mediating between goals that are immediately attainable and ultimate, ideal and less-than-ideal. Policy goals epitomize a society's "belief systems" or "interpretative systems," as Huxley calls them,[11] and serve as a sort of beacon to guide thinking about policy decisions. All participants in policy-making bring to it, consciously or unconsciously, their individual belief systems as reference points. The student needs to know the premises of the knowledge, values and

---

[10] Daniel Lerner and Harold D. Lasswell, eds. *The Policy Sciences: Recent Developments in Scope and Method* (Stanford, Cal.: Stanford University Press, 1951), ix.
[11] Huxley, *op. cit.*, 4.

norms which constitute social work's belief system, and be able to assess policy goals in the light of this belief system and its difference from those of other groups in society.

In this connection, relevant theory about reference groups helps explain the formation of belief systems. Hickman and Kuhn's study suggests the relative importance of beliefs derived from reference groups. They delineate three main layers of a person's belief system.[12] The first consists of the old historic beliefs of the larger society as handed down by church and school. A second layer consists of currently dominant beliefs as purveyed by the mass communications media. The third layer derives from those groups of people who "matter" to a person and thereby constitute his "significant" referents. Beliefs derived from such reference groups mediate and define the beliefs derived from other sources. However, since a person identifies with several reference groups and these may hold incompatible beliefs, he must choose from among them. He makes his choice on the basis of how he ranks the groups in relation to his most highly valued statuses and roles.[13]

The professional social worker specifically brings to policy-making the goals of social welfare and social work. These need to be clarified with the student.[14] An interesting formulation of social welfare beliefs, inferred from analysis of social welfare provisions made by a large American community, sets forth these major goal categories: (1) assurance of minimum necessities for decent living; (2) maintenance and improvement of physical and mental health; (3) improvement of social relations and social responsibility; and (4) enrichment of life and enjoyment of leisure through recreational and cultural pursuits.[15] The social work emphasis is suggested by *The Nature of Social Work*, which defines the basic commitments of the profession. The student needs to be impressed with his responsibility for interpreting positively both social welfare and social work viewpoints, and for "standing up to be counted" in times of criticism and challenge.

---

12 Hickman and Kuhn, *op. cit.*, 176–177.
13 *Ibid.*, 159–161.
14 The report of the Curriculum Study project on values and ethics suggests desirable curriculum objectives.
15 *The Resources-Needs Study: A Report of the First Phase of the Project* (Philadelphia: Health and Welfare Council of Philadelphia, 1956).

Objective XIII:

$$\left.\begin{array}{l}\text{UNDERSTANDING,}\\\text{ASSESSING, AND}\\\text{VIEWING PROFESSIONALLY}\end{array}\right\}\text{POLICY}\left\{\begin{array}{l}\text{AS}\\\text{MANIFESTING}\\\text{THE POSSIBLE}\end{array}\right.$$

In mediating between the immediately attainable and the ultimate, the policy-making process must take into consideration the possible as well as the desirable. Stating the problem of ascertaining the possible from the standpoint of social work, Lester B. Granger had this to say:

> Manifestation of basic human needs may vary according to basic living conditions, but social work's undeviating responsibility is to meet those needs wherever they are found, with the best services that circumstances afford, rather than to theorize about how conditions should be in some near-ideal environment. How far is "possible"? As far as human ingenuity, backed by social consciousness, can distribute those services which the community can make available. Each community, in the last analysis, must determine "how far is possible"— must establish its own priorities, whether on a federal, state or local basis.[16]

The student should recognize that ends and means have no simple correlation. Today the problem of ascertaining the possible depends primarily upon political, economic and legal capability factors. For, in the phrase of MacIver and Knight, these constitute the "means structures" of modern society.[17] They need to be used by the citizen in pursuit of his goals, but must not be regarded as goals in themselves. The student should understand that each of these means structures is a power system representing danger to the individual to the extent that its powers go unchecked. For understanding the *politically* possible, the student needs to grasp the meaning of Justice Felix Frankfurter's aphorism that "Our democracy presupposes the deliberative process as a condition of

[16] Lester B. Granger, "Basic Human Needs" in *Social Service and the Standards of Living, Proceedings* of the Sixth International Conference of Social Work, Madras, December 12-19, 1952 (Bombay, India: The South-East Regional Office, International Conference of Social Work, 1952), 46.

[17] Robert M. MacIver, *Democracy and the Economic Challenge* (New York: Alfred A. Knopf, Inc., 1952); Frank H. Knight, *Freedom and Reform* (New York: Harper and Brothers, 1947).

thought and of responsible choice by the electorate." A democracy requires that the people themselves shall determine policy goals and criteria, although the specialized work of policy formulation is entrusted to representative groups. The student should become aware of influences brought to bear upon the democratic process in terms of such concepts as power, countervailing power, power centers, and power conflicts. He should gain familiarity with the epochal political movements of the past which introduced new climates for social welfare policy-making, the contributions of the major political parties to social welfare in the past, and their current positions on social welfare issues.

Understanding the concept of "positive government" in relation to governmental assumption of welfare responsibilities is crucial. The student should recognize the falsehood of the "either-or" antithesis.

> Either-or? Liberty *or* governmental intervention? Liberty *or* servitude? Liberty without governmental interference *or* loss of liberty when government in any way enters into our economic affairs, into our health programs, into our philanthropic activities? The intransigence of this *either or* bedevils the solution of many problems. It is so unrealistic, so wholly unrelated to the evidence.[18]

It is also important to comprehend and develop conviction about the concept of government as a service institution in society. The student should understand the implication that the resort to governmental social welfare represents a sharp break from the idea of using government merely as a policing institution:

> Social security has come to be sought not in the discipline of the workhouses and the standardized rigors of less eligibility; not in those loathed negatives of the principles of 1834, but in the positive affirmatives of the substance of welfare.[19]

In considering what is *economically* possible, it must be impressed upon the student that in modern society political and economic

[18] Robert M. MacIver, "Government and Social Welfare" in *National Policies for Education, Health and Social Services,* ed. James E. Russell (Garden City: Doubleday & Company, 1955), 524.
[19] Beales, *op. cit.,* 22.

considerations often "interpenetrate." [20] The American and Canadian economies are frequently described as "mixed" economies, meaning that they involve close cooperation between government and private enterprise. The student should be aware of government's influence upon our economy through its assumption of considerable responsibility for the growth and stability of the economy, for promoting justice, and for safeguarding and raising living standards.

The swift economic evolution of modern times should be understood with particular reference to the impact of two massive historical movements: the growth of industrialization and the rising expectations of people everywhere for a fair share of its fruits, in goods and services. The student should understand the interrelation of wants, resources and the technology by which resources are converted to meeting human needs; also, the influence of productivity upon the allocation of goods and services. "Decent, humane feelings have a chance to function in effective terms in proportion to our productivity. We will be increasingly ashamed of want in our society as it becomes more and more obvious that it is unnecessary." [21]

The tax and financing policies on which support of social welfare programs rests must be understood in their relation to maintenance and improvement of social welfare service. In this connection the different approaches to social welfare of labor, management and agriculture must be understood; also the way in which the community development concept translates democracy into world socio-economic terms.

Consideration of the *legally* possible involves an understanding of the purpose and function of law in a democratic society. This has been succinctly stated by Roscoe Pound in his speech for Law Day USA, 1958, "The law is the highest inheritance the sovereign people has, for without the law there would be no sovereign people and no inheritance." [22] The student should understand that law provides a structure of rights and obligations, immunities and

20 James M. Clark, "America's Changing Capitalism: The Interplay of Politics and Economics" in *Freedom and Control in Modern Society*, ed. Morroe Berger (New York: D. Van Nostrand Company, Inc., 1954).
21 Robert M. Ball, "Social Security Today," *Public Welfare*, XV (July, 1957), 87.
22 Quoted in *Time*, May 5, 1958.

exposures, privileges and disabilities, within which social inter-
actions take place. This structure is constantly changing:

> As interpersonal contacts increase and become more casual and fleet-
> ing, as population density grows and as individual or group interests
> proliferate, law functions in more and more areas where less formal
> controls previously sufficed to maintain the conditions of social order
> and the protection of society's manifold interests.[23]

Law should be viewed as a flexible, adaptable means of authoriz-
ing and sanctioning social welfare measures. The student should
be familiar with basic legal concepts and principles which assert
human rights and define human relations; with the general functions and organizational procedure of the judicial system; with the
nature of judicial decisions; and with the concept of judicial review as a test of constitutionality. Ability to read and understand
statutes, law cases and judicial decisions needs to be developed, as
well as familiarity with law enforcement machinery, the relationships of lawyers and social workers, and the kinds of problems
which require professional help from lawyers or legal aid services.

The student should acquire understanding of major pieces of
legislation upon which modern social welfare is built, such as the
Social Security Act, Mental Health Act and similar legislation in
other social welfare areas.

Objective XIV:

UNDERSTANDING,			AS POSING
INTERPRETING, AND	}	POLICY {	SOCIAL
VIEWING PROFESSIONALLY			ISSUES

This objective further emphasizes the concept of *policy* as continually changing and draws attention to the social worker's need
to be alert to changing concerns, conditions and climates of opinion which place existing policy at issue. It assumes that the social
worker must be capable of making informed and considered judgments about the issues at the growing edges of *policy,* to guide his
own activity and that of others who turn to him for advice on
social welfare matters.

[23] Berger, *op. cit.,* 191.

The student should develop a "nose for issues."He needs ability to assess issues in the interest of social work and the whole field of social welfare and to arrive at professional positions concertedly with other social workers through organized professional machinery. He will need to develop also the skills of affirming and defending professional policy positions, for, as Aneurin Bevan recently remarked, "Silence is not an effective instrument in a democracy."

The student should acquire knowledge of major issues currently before the profession and the field, and should be encouraged to try his hand at formulating positions appropriate for the profession to take in light of its philosophy and functions.

Objective XV:

$$\left.\begin{array}{l} \text{UNDERSTANDING,} \\ \text{INTERPRETING, AND} \\ \text{VIEWING PROFESSIONALLY} \end{array}\right\} \text{POLICY} \left\{\begin{array}{l} \text{AS} \\ \text{SOCIAL} \\ \text{ACTION} \end{array}\right.$$

This objective aims to impress upon the student that social action is the purpose of all policy activity. As Chief Justice Oliver Wendell Holmes averred in one of his opinions, "To act is to affirm the worth of an end."

The student must develop knowledge of the forces of resistance and acceptance, and their part in changing attitudes and opinions on social welfare matters. He needs to understand that his role in social action may involve advocacy of or opposition to change, depending upon the nature of the proposals. Fundamentally it will involve application of the art of persuasion, which one of its most gifted practitioners has called "the art of the engineering of consent." [24] This art of engineering consent is one of those universal arts within everybody's competence to some extent, but the student will need some working knowledge of its technical aspects, such as mapping strategy and choosing appropriate tactics.

[24] Edward L. Bernays (ed.), *The Engineering of Consent* (Norman: University of Oklahoma Press, 1955).

CHAPTER VII

Recommended Curriculum Objectives in Regard to Social Welfare Provision

It will be recalled that the term *provision* was defined in Chapter III:

> As used here, the term *provision* connotes the popular idea of making things available that are needed or desired. More technically, the term is intended to connote ways of meeting social welfare problems or of implementing social welfare policy. It may take the form of programs, services, agencies, and personnel. As components of the concept *provision,* each of these forms must be viewed in its historical, philosophical, legal, and community contexts.

Required courses in the social services sequence now emphasize content of this nature to an extent that often tends to neglect adequate attention to concepts of *problem* and *policy.* As was noted in Chapter II, these courses usually focus on selected programs, primarily tax-supported ones, and give detailed consideration to facts about their legislative background, historical development, financial and administrative structures, and operational formulas for determining eligibility and benefit rates.

The set of objectives listed below is aimed at a better balance between *provision* content and content about *problem* and *policy.* The objectives emphasize the structural-functional aspects of the provision of social welfare services. They include content on administration and community organization which all social workers need to know and understand, to be elaborated upon in the methods courses. Each objective highlights one of these concepts about *provision:*

1. *Provision* consists of the mobilized resources of society.
2. *Provision* is organized in the social agency.
3. *Provision* is client-centered service.

4. *Provision* is work performed in team relationships.

5. *Provision* is geared to serving the total community.

Objective XVI:

UNDERSTANDING,
ASSESSING, AND
VIEWING PROFESSIONALLY } PROVISION { AS
MOBILIZED RESOURCES
OF SOCIETY

The aim of this objective is to draw attention to the role of society as provider of resources for social welfare service. An understanding of the concept of resources as wide-ranged and varied is crucial if the student is to gain a clear conception of society's role as provider. The student should be helped to assess the adequacy of social welfare resources in the context of the resources that are known and potential within the individual himself, within his circle of family, friends, and neighbors as well as within the institutions of society. To understand the uneven development of social welfare provision in different places in the world and the nation, the student needs to recognize and assess the influence of differing social needs, social conditions, interests, ideologies, and technological developments.

The differing capability of societies, or political or geographical segments thereof, to mobilize social welfare resources requires knowledge of the economic factors, in view of the predominantly industrialized, money economy of our society. It would seem especially important to understand the relation of trends in production, employment and income to the scope and adequacy of the provision of social welfare services. Vital to understanding the financing of social welfare provisions is recognition that social welfare claims upon the total national income must compete not only with personal consumption preferences, but also with a wide range of general welfare programs upon which high valuations are placed.

Because the concept of social welfare tends to be as limitless as human aspirations, but resources are often viewed as limited, the student needs to understand and develop professional conviction about the importance of planning in the development of resources for social welfare purposes. He needs to understand the concept of planning as the weighing and balancing of human needs and re-

sources toward accomplishing desired goals and should be familiar
with the consequences of planlessness as evidenced by the neglect
of important categories of need, either because of their lack of
popular appeal or lack of sufficient knowledge about them.

Planning for social welfare development should be viewed as
part of total community development.[1] Familiarity with the major
types of community planning programs at local, state, national,
and international levels [2] will be needed.

Since planning involves the allocation of community resources,
the problem of priorities is often posed. It is essential that the student understand some of the criteria employed in establishing
priorities [3] and the major factors which enter into setting different
priorities for short-run, intermediate and long-run developments.
Appropriate solution levels, such as those sloganized by the phrase
"much for care, more for cure, most for prevention," should be
explored with the student in this connection.

Objective XVII:

$$\left.\begin{array}{l}\text{UNDERSTANDING,}\\\text{ASSESSING, AND}\\\text{VIEWING PROFESSIONALLY}\end{array}\right\}\text{PROVISION}\left\{\begin{array}{l}\text{AS}\\\text{AGENCY}\\\text{ORGANIZED}\end{array}\right.$$

This objective lays stress on the social agency as a component in
the provision of social welfare services. It implies that the student
preparing for professional practice needs to be knowledgeable
about the nature and theory of administrative organization for
social welfare and alert to the factors that significantly influence
professional performance and often determine what professional
services are to be offered, to whom, and toward what service ends.[4]

The social agency is an organization sanctioned by society, deriv-
ing its functions from society and representing the organized con-

1 Norman Collison, *Report on Concepts and Principles of Community Development.*
(New York: National Social Welfare Assembly, 1957). Mimeographed.
2 Paul C. Phillips, *Trends in Community Development Programs in the United States.*
(Washington, D.C.: International Cooperation Administration, February, 1958).
Processed.
3 George James, "Changing Priorities in Public Health," *Public Health Reports*
(July, 1956).
4 Herbert A. Simon, *Administrative Behavior: A Study of the Decision-Making Proc-*
esses in Administrative Organization, 2nd ed. (New York: The Macmillan Company,
1957).

cern of society for all people. The characteristics of the agency as a corporate entity must be understood, and that, as a public instrument, the agency is answerable to the people for its performance. In view of the professional character of agency service, research must be recognized as a major instrument of accountability.

> In an earlier era the profession could justify itself by its intentions and activities; today we have the right to ask for systematic validation by measurement of effects and/or evaluation of the process by which service is undertaken.[5]

The social agency is an organization of ways and means by which agency functions are "translated into provisions of help." [6] The student needs to understand the various types of administrative organization and to assess the appropriateness of administrative structures to the professional service functions of the agency. He should learn the principles of structuring authority-responsibility within the agency, with regard to leadership and competence components; [7] also the principles of structuring communication, to insure a proper flow of information, instructions and reports and transmittal of the agency "culture" to all posts within the organization and to outside points of contact. The importance of control structures must be emphasized, not as ends in themselves, but as means to maximum accomplishment of agency objectives.

Finally, the student needs to understand the dynamics of organizational change, with respect to redefinition of objectives, acceptance or rejection of new functions, and restructuring of the work organization.[8]

Objective XVIII:

UNDERSTANDING, ASSESSING, AND VIEWING PROFESSIONALLY } PROVISION { AS CLIENT-CENTERED SERVICE

The fact that the primary function of a social agency is to help people with their problems must be kept uppermost in thinking

[5] Alfred Kahn, "Research Planning: Facilitating Social Work Research," *Social Service Review*, XXX (September 1956), 331.
[6] Perlman, *op. cit.*, 45.
[7] Robert Bierstedt, "The Problem of Authority" in Berger, *op. cit.*, 67–81.
[8] Lippitt, *et al.*, *op. cit.*

about *provision* of social welfare services. The administration of the agency program must be viewed from the standpoint of the service objectives. The student should be familiar with the standards and requirements essential to effective performance of agency services, distinguishing the social work services by recognizing that social work concerns itself with enhancing the social functioning of individuals, groups, and communities. The professional nature of the agency's social work function needs to be assessed with the student in terms of the varied knowledge that feeds it, the ethical commitments which imbue it, the goals that guide it, and the skills which empower it.

For the agency to render service of high quality, efficiency and promptness, there must be proper recruitment, deployment and utilization of a staff sufficient in number and quality to achieve service objectives. The student should see recruitment principles as related to performance requirements and should be encouraged to examine his own interest in a social work career in terms of his motivations and expectations and the special problems of working in social work.[9] Working in social work, as in anything else, is a means of earning a livelihood and therefore requires learning how to protect and advance one's economic interests commensurate with a professional status. The student should acquire knowledge of desirable personnel policies and practices in social work administration, and develop ability to assess an agency as a desirable place in which to work.

It is important to think about deployment and utilization of staff also in terms of the requirements for effective service. A division of work is needed that makes the fullest use of individual skills and capacities and best handles the time and space complexities of work. The student should learn to view the social work job as part of a network of interrelated jobs in the agency, each job dependent upon the other and none really possible of accomplishment without the other. Likewise he needs to recognize that the structures, policies, standards, and procedures of the agency "give form, order-

[9] Charlotte G. Babcock, "Social Work as Work," *Social Casework*, XXXIV (December, 1953).

liness, consistency and dependable movement"[10] to the agency's services, as well as provide the criteria for evaluating performance and holding both worker and agency accountable to the public.

Objective XIX:

$$
\left.
\begin{array}{l}
\text{UNDERSTANDING,} \\
\text{INTERPRETING, AND} \\
\text{VIEWING PROFESSIONALLY}
\end{array}
\right\}
\text{PROVISION}
\left\{
\begin{array}{l}
\text{AS} \\
\text{TEAM} \\
\text{WORK}
\end{array}
\right.
$$

The effective performance of a social work service requires contributions from the total personnel of the agency in terms of individual responsibilities and functions. It is therefore important to understand the integrative purpose of the social agency as an instrument of work organization.

The student needs to understand how work is integrated and coordinated in the agency through a system of work roles and relationships, defined and controlled by the agency objectives, policies, standards, and structures of authority and responsibility, line and staff functioning, communication, and training. The basic roles which the professional practitioner carries as a member of the agency staff must be understood, particularly the roles of employe, professional worker, co-worker, and agency representative in interagency and community relations. Also the student should understand the major roles which other personnel in the agency carry, and how his expectation of their role performance influences his own role performance in such areas of agency activity as policy-making, management, supervision, consultation, office management, and interagency and community relations.

The integration of the work of the agency often involves group, as well as individual, relationships among agency personnel. The student should understand the nature and process of group activity within the agency in dealing with routine or special problems or projects. He should develop a working knowledge of committee management and the dynamics of group deliberation, discussion and decision-making.[11]

[10] Perlman, *op. cit.*, 49.
[11] Grace L. Coyle and Margaret E. Hartford, *Social Process in the Community and the Group* (New York: Council on Social Work and Education, 1958), 83–85.

Objective XX:

UNDERSTANDING,			AS GEARED TO
ASSESSING, AND	} PROVISION {	SERVING THE
VIEWING PROFESSIONALLY			TOTAL COMMUNITY

It is the aim of this objective to reinforce the picture of the agency as a component part of a community's institutionalized network of services to people. The student needs to view agency function and role performance in the context of community systems of social welfare services and professions, at local, state, national, and international levels. As a social worker, he may be called to serve anywhere in the country and the world and needs therefore to have the knowledge of differing patterns and stages of development of social welfare organization in order to make appropriate adjustments.

It is also important to know that agencies are interdependent and interrelated in their activity, displaying at once unique and common features, determined by their origin and growth; their concept and content of service; the auspices under which they operate; the kind of clientele they hold themselves responsible to serve; the various professional, non-professional and volunteer staff they use; and the kind of community in which they function, especially in such characteristics as size, composition and cultural structures. Viewing the agency in relation to other agencies in the community involves professional concern for comprehensiveness and balance of services provided, for coordination and cooperation among agencies and for maximum coverage of need and quality of service.

To view the agency in its community context, the student should identify and assess the community conditions and attitudes which affect agency operations, recognizing that, as a community function, the provision of social welfare services must respond to human needs, conditions and feelings within the community. Also he must understand and develop professional conviction about agency and professional responsibility not only to help people with their problems, but to help the community itself to respond more effectively to changing human needs, interests, conditions, and ideologies. The role of the profession as a "change agent" must be understood.[12] Agency and profession have a responsibility to bring their relevant experience and knowledge to bear upon community processes of "planned change." [13] Principles particularly appropriate to the social work approach to creating, changing and coordinating social welfare functions and structures, for better service to the total community, need to be explored with the student.[14]

[12] Lippitt *et al., op. cit.*
[13] *Ibid.*
[14] Murray G. Ross, "Conceptual Problems in Community Organization," *Social Service Review*, XXX (June 1956); see also his *Community Organization: Theory and Principles* (New York: Harper and Brothers, 1955).

CHAPTER VIII

Summary

This project, as part of the larger Curriculum Study, has been concerned with the same question to which the whole Study was addressed: What are the desirable curriculum objectives for social work education? The project confined its inquiry to one of the three major content areas of the present professional curriculum, termed "The Social Services" in the current *Curriculum Policy Statement.*

The focus on desirable objectives excluded consideration of other important aspects of curriculum. No attempt was made to deal with learning experiences for achieving objectives, nor to indicate any organization of objectives into course sequences. Methods and means of evaluating students were not considered.

A survey was made of the nature of current course offerings in the social services content area which revealed that the present content lacks cohesiveness and focus on basic professional content. In general, current offerings were found to be more often diffuse than concentrated, fragmentary than integrated, factual than conceptual, and descriptive than analytical. These findings posed the specific questions to which the project attempted to find answers:

What content would provide a balanced and cohesive description of the subject area?

What concepts would bring the content into an appropriate professional and graduate educational focus?

What behavior should the student be expected to develop in learning this content?

What would be the best way of stating as curriculum objectives the content and the behavior expectations?

In arriving at answers, the project director was guided by procedures set in the overall Curriculum Study design. These focused on: (1) content analysis of a wide variety of curricular materials, professional literature and related social science writings; (2) field visits to selected schools of social work for interviews with faculty members and conferences with curriculum committees; and (3) consultation from a selected group of educators and practitioners organized in an advisory panel.

As study proceeded, a frame of reference for selecting desirable curriculum objectives emerged. It provided six components as selection criteria:

1. A rationale for stating curriculum objectives—that curriculum objectives are educationally most useful when stated in terms of the content to be imparted and the behavior to result from student learning of specified content.

2. An orienting educational philosophy—that curriculum objectives best serve the profession of social work when most compatible with defined social work values, goals, functions, and activities.

3. A focusing point of view—that curriculum objectives in this content area have most professional relevance and significance when the content is approached institutionally from the standpoint of society's organized responses to human needs.

4. An anchoring term of reference—that curriculum objectives around institutional content have greatest social work usefulness when focused upon the institutional aspects which express society's organized concern for the well-being of its members as individuals and in family and community groups—*social welfare.*

5. A unifying set of concepts—that curriculum objectives around social welfare content can best be attained when the content is conceptualized in descriptive and analytical terms, here embodied in seven specifically defined major concepts.

6. An intellectually challenging approach—that curriculum objectives in the social welfare content area can best contribute to a graduate level of education when the content makes intellectual demands on the student to be critical and thoughtful.

As unifying concepts, three "core knowledge" concepts were identified for use in selecting relevant social welfare content to be organized into the social work curriculum:

Problem—defined as referring to phenomena which bring under scrutiny society's institutional provisions for meeting needs.

Policy—defined as referring to a formulated course of action in relation to a problem.

Provision—defined as referring to ways of meeting problems or implementing policy in the form of programs, services, agencies, and personnel.

Analysis of the nature and relationships of these "core knowledge" concepts in a way meaningful for social work was thought to require searching inquiry centering around four additional "analytical" concepts:

Rights—to examine the core knowledge content by raising questions that identify its "ought" elements. The concept rests upon the value social work places upon the individuality and integrity of the human being.

Responsibility—to examine the core knowledge content by questions that identify its "should" elements. This concept rests on recognition of the interdependence of the various units of society and the society as a whole.

Capability—to examine the core knowledge content by questions that identify "can" elements in the forces and resources available in society.

Role—to examine the core content by raising questions that identify its "must" elements, with respect to action appropriate to persons and groups, particularly social work practitioners.

The student's study of the substantive concepts in light of the analytical concepts (the content aspect of the educational objectives) was expected to develop student behaviors of "knowing," "doing," and "feeling" (the behavioral aspects of the objectives). Two subcategories of behaviors were identified under "knowing," two under "doing," and three under "feeling." Similarly, a total of twenty subconcepts were identified in the three "core knowledge" concepts.

The recommended objectives suggested the desirability of a change of title for this content area of the curriculum. SOCIAL WELFARE POLICY AND SERVICES was believed to be the one most descriptive of the content covered and the graduate level at which it was to be offered.

In summary, the project recommends as objectives for required courses in this curriculum area specified student behaviors in relation to a set of concepts that emphasize the organization, administration and change aspects of social welfare functions and structures in a democratic society.

The organization aspects focus on social welfare problems and contemporary solutions. The student would learn to identify the functional and structural requisites for social welfare in a modern society. Stress would be placed on the major programs and professions representing contemporary solutions of major problems, and on analysis of their main features from historical, philosophical and comparative standpoints. The effectiveness and adequacy of the major solutions would be assessed in terms of modern conceptions of human rights, social responsibility, professional role, and society's capability potentials. The development of social work as a social institution and its problem-solving functions and goals would be highlighted.

The administration aspects focus on knowledge, skill and attitudes important as preparation for the beginning practitioner's involvement in agency practice. They would make explicit the fact that social work services are provided largely through a social agency; the nature of the social agency; the social worker's involvement in administering and influencing agency policy and services, especially in the typical roles assumed by the professional practitioner as a member of an agency staff and as the agency representative in outside contacts.

The change aspect of the content is bi-focal, emphasizing worker involvement in community organization for social welfare and in social policy and action. The community organization content would explore the process of planned change by which communities create, coordinate and change their social welfare functions and structures. It would identify as social work components of community organization the special problems which social work functions and structures center upon. The social policy and action content would focus on the professional obligation to evaluate social institutions and guide institutional change by democratic methods. It would analyze and make explicit the assumptions underlying formulated and proposed social policy goals of the profession and other groups, and would involve the student in assessing the factual bases, the possibilities, the strategy, and the tactics of professional action to influence policy development in governmental and nongovernmental institutional structures.

This summary of curriculum objectives cannot be properly concluded without reiteration that the objectives can be realized only insofar as the learning experiences of the student encourage speculation, investigation, analysis, discussion, and decision-making.

Selected Bibliography

The bibliography below lists publications mentioned in the text together with additional publications to which this report is in debt. The multiple focus of many of the publications made impracticable a division of the bibliographies into sections on problem, policy and provision.

Abbott, Edith. *Social Welfare and Professional Education*, rev. ed. Chicago: University of Chicago Press, 1942.

Alexander, Chauncey A. and McCann, Charles M. "The Concept of Representativeness in Community Organization," *Social Work*, 1 (January 1956).

American Assembly, The. *Economic Security for Americans*. Third Assembly, Arden House, Harriman, N.Y. New York: Columbia University, Graduate School of Business, 1954.

American Association of Schools of Social Work. *Education for the Public Social Services*. Chapel Hill: University of North Carolina Press, 1942.

American Association of Social Workers. *Social Workers in 1950: Report of a Study of Salaries and Working Conditions*. New York: Association Press, 1952.

American Council of Learned Societies. *Government under Law and the Individual*. New York: American Council of Learned Societies, 1957.

American Political Science Association. *Goals for Political Science*. New York: William Sloane Associates, 1951.

Appleby, Paul H. *Morality and Administration in Democratic Government*. Baton Rouge: Louisiana State University Press, 1952.

———. *Policy and Administration*. Birmingham: University of Alabama Press, 1949.

Aron, Raymond and Heckscher, August. *Diversity of Worlds*. New York: Reynal & Company, 1957.

Arrow, Kenneth J. *Social Choice and Individual Values*. Cowles Commission for Research in Economics, Monograph No. 12. New York: John Wiley & Sons, 1951.

Ascher, Charles S. *et al. Urban Redevelopment*, ed. Coleman Woodbury. Chicago: University of Chicago Press, 1953.

Asher, Robert E. *et al. United Nations and Economic and Social Co-operation.* Washington, D.C.: The Brookings Institution, 1957.

Babcock, Charlotte G. "Social Work as Work," *Social Casework,* XXXIV (December 1953).

Bachmann, E. Theodore (ed.). *Churches and Social Welfare,* Volume III: *The Emerging Perspective: Response and Prospect.* New York: National Council of the Churches of Christ in the U.S.A., 1956.

Bailey, Stephen K. *Congress at Work.* New York: Henry Holt and Company, 1952.

————. *Congress Makes a Law.* New York: Columbia University Press, 1950.

Bales, Robert F. "In Conference," *Harvard Business Review,* 32.

Ball, Robert M. "Social Security Today," *Public Welfare,* XV (July 1957).

Barnes, Harry Elmer and Ruedi, O. M. *The American Way of Life: Our Institutional Patterns and Social Problems.* New York: Prentice-Hall, 1942.

Bayliff, Russell E. *et al. Values and Policy in American Society.* Dubuque, Iowa: William C. Brown Co., 1954.

Beales, Hugh L. *The Making of Social Policy.* L. T. Hobhouse Memorial Trust Lecture. Oxford: The Clarendon Press, 1946.

Berger, Morroe (ed.). *Freedom and Control in Modern Society.* New York: D. Van Nostrand Company, 1954.

Berle, A. A. *The 20th Century Capitalist Revolution.* New York: Harcourt, Brace and Company, 1954.

Bernard, Jessie S. *Social Problems at Midcentury: Role, Status and Stress in a Context of Abundance.* New York: The Dryden Press, 1957.

Bernays, Edward L. (ed.). *The Engineering of Consent.* Norman: University of Oklahoma Press, 1955.

Beveridge, Sir William H. *Social Insurance and Allied Services.* New York: The Macmillan Company, 1942.

Biddle, William W. *The Cultivation of Community Leaders.* New York: Harper and Brothers, 1953.

Bierstedt, Robert. "The Problem of Authority" in *Freedom and Control in Modern Society,* ed. Morroe Berger. New York: D. Van Nostrand Company, 1954.

Bisno, Herbert. *The Philosophy of Social Work.* Washington, D.C.: Public Affairs Press, 1952.

Blau, Peter M. *The Dynamics of Bureaucracy.* Chicago: University of Chicago Press, 1955.

Blauch, Lloyd E. (ed.). *Education for the Professions.* U.S. Department of Health, Education, and Welfare, Office of Education. Washington, D.C.: Government Printing Office, 1955.

Bloch, Herbert A. *Disorganization, Personal and Social.* New York: Alfred A. Knopf, 1952.

Bloom, Benjamin S. (ed.). *Taxonomy of Educational Objectives.* New York: Longmans, Green and Co., 1956.

Bloomfield, Lincoln P. *Evolution or Revolution.* Cambridge: Harvard University Press, 1957.

Boulding, Kenneth E. *The Image: Knowledge in Life and Society.* Ann Arbor: University of Michigan Press, 1956.

————. *Principles of Economic Policy.* Englewood Cliffs, N.J.: Prentice-Hall, 1958.

Bremner, Robert H. *From the Depths: The Discovery of Poverty in the United States.* New York: New York University Press, 1956.

Bruner, Jerome S. *et al. A Study of Thinking.* New York: John Wiley & Sons, 1956.

Bruno, Frank J. *Trends in Social Work, 1874–1956,* 2nd ed. New York: Columbia University Press, 1957.

Buell, Bradley *et al. Community Planning for Human Services.* New York: Columbia University Press, 1952.

Burns, Eveline M. *Social Security and Public Policy.* New York: McGraw-Hill Book Company, 1956.

Caplow, Theodore. *The Sociology of Work.* Minneapolis: University of Minnesota Press, 1954.

Carlston, Kenneth S. *Law and Structures of Social Action.* New York: Columbia University Press, 1956.

Carr-Saunders, A. M. and Wilson, P. A. *The Professions.* Oxford: The Clarendon Press, 1933.

Carter, Genevieve W. "Practice Theory in Community Organization," *Social Work,* 3 (April 1958).

Case, Clarence M. "What Is a Social Problem?" in *Analyzing Social Problems,* ed. John Eric Nordskog *et al.* New York: The Dryden Press, 1950.

Castro, Josué de. *The Geography of Hunger.* Boston: Little, Brown & Company, 1951.

Catlin, George. *On Political Goals.* New York: St. Martin's Press, 1957.

Chapin, Stuart F. *Contemporary American Institutions.* New York: Harper and Brothers, 1935.

Clark, James M. "America's Changing Capitalism: The Interplay of Politics and Economics" in *Freedom and Control in Modern Soci-*

ety, ed Morroe Berger. New York: D. Van Nostrand Company, 1954.

Clark, John Maurice. *Economic Institutions and Human Welfare.* New York: Alfred A. Knopf, 1957.

Cloward, R. A. "Agency Structure as a Variable in Services to Groups" in *Group Work and Community Organization.* New York: Columbia University Press, 1956.

Cockerill, Eleanor. "The Interdependence of the Professions in Helping People," *Social Casework,* XXXIV (November 1953).

Cohen, Nathan E. *Social Work in the American Tradition.* New York: The Dryden Press, 1958.

Corson, John J. and McConnell, J. W. *Economic Needs of Older People.* New York: Twentieth Century Fund, 1956.

Coser, Lewis A. *The Functions of Social Conflict.* Glencoe, Ill.: The Free Press, 1956.

Coyle, Grace L. "New Insights Available to the Social Worker from Social Sciences," *Social Service Review,* XXVI (September 1952).

———. "The Social Worker and His Society," *Social Service Review,* XXVI (December 1952).

——— and Hartford, Margaret E. *Social Process in the Community and the Group.* New York: Council on Social Work Education, 1958.

Cuber, John F. and Kenkel, William F. *Social Stratification in the United States.* New York: Appleton-Century-Crofts, 1954.

Dahl, Robert A. and Lindblom, Charles E. *Politics, Economics and Welfare.* New York: Harper and Brothers, 1953.

Davis, Donald K. *et al. Education for Professional Responsibility.* Report of the Proceedings of the Inter-Professions Conference on Education for Professional Responsibility, Buck Hill Falls, Pa., 1948. Pittsburgh: The Carnegie Press, 1948 (available from Rutgers University Press, New Brunswick, N.J.).

Davis, Michael M. *Medical Care for Tomorrow.* New York: Harper and Brothers, 1955.

DeJongh, J. F. "Self-Help in Modern Society," *Social Work Journal,* XXXV (October 1954).

de Schweinitz, Karl. "Social Values and Social Action—the Intellectual Base as Illustrated in the Study of History," *Social Service Review,* XXX (June 1956).

Dewhurst, J. Frederic and Associates. *America's Needs and Resources: A New Survey.* New York: Twentieth Century Fund, 1955.

Dressel, Paul L. and Mayhew, Lewis B. *General Education: Explora-*

tions in Evaluation. Washington, D.C.: American Council on Education, 1954.

Edel, Abraham. *Ethical Judgment: The Use of Science in Ethics.* Glencoe, Ill.: The Free Press, 1955.

Einzig, Paul. *The Economic Consequences of Automation.* New York: W. W. Norton and Company, 1956.

Eulau, Heinz *et al.* (eds.). *Political Behavior.* Glencoe, Ill.: The Free Press, 1956.

Eyden, Joan. "Social Services in the Modern State," *Case Conference* (February 1955).

Family Service Association of America. *Scope and Methods of the Family Service Agency.* New York: Family Service Association of America, 1953.

Feibelman, James *The Institutions of Society.* London: George Allen and Unwin, 1956.

Fein, Rashi. *Economics of Mental Health.* New York: Joint Commission on Mental Illness and Health, 1958.

Feldman, Frances L. *The Family in a Money World.* New York: Family Service Association of America, 1957.

Ferguson, Virginia S. "Fifty Years of Social Work" in *The Social Welfare Forum, 1950,* published for the National Conference of Social Work. New York: Columbia University Press, 1950.

Fine, Sidney. *Laissez Faire and the General-Welfare State: A Study of Conflict in American Thought, 1865–1901.* Ann Arbor: University of Michigan Press, 1956.

Foote, Nelson N. and Cottrell, Leonard S., Jr. *Identity and Interpersonal Competence: A New Direction in Family Research.* Chicago: University of Chicago Press, 1955.

Francis, Roy G. and Stone, Robert C. *Service and Procedure in Bureaucracy.* Minneapolis: University of Minnesota Press, 1956.

Frank, Lawrence K. *Society as the Patient: Essays on Culture and Personality.* New Brunswick: Rutgers University Press, 1948.

Freeman, John S. *The Political Process: Executive Bureau–Legislative Committee Relations.* Garden City, N.Y.: Doubleday & Co., 1955.

Friedlander, Walter A. *Introduction to Social Welfare.* New York: Prentice-Hall, 1955.

Fuller, Richard C. "Sociological Theory and Social Problems" in *Analyzing Social Problems,* ed. John Eric Nordskog *et al.* New York: The Dryden Press, 1950.

Gillin, John L. *Social Problems.* New York: Appleton-Century-Crofts, 1952.

Glick, Paul C. *American Families.* New York: John Wiley & Sons, 1957.

Granger, Lester B. "Basic Human Needs" in *Social Service and the Standards of Living.* Proceedings of the Sixth International Conference of Social Work, Madras, December 12–19, 1952. Bombay, India: The South-East Regional Office, International Conference of Social Work, 1952.

Greenwood, Ernest. "Attributes of a Profession," *Social Work,* 2 (July 1957).

Gross, Neal C. *et al. Explorations in Role Analysis: Studies of the School Superintendency Role.* New York: John Wiley & Sons, 1958.

Gurvitch, Georgil D. and Moore, Wilbert E. (eds.). *Twentieth Century Sociology.* New York: The Philosophical Library, 1945.

Gwynn, John M. *Curriculum Principles and Social Trends.* New York: The Macmillan Company, 1950.

Hall, Everett W. *Modern Science and Human Values: A Study in the History of Ideas.* New York: D. Van Nostrand Company, 1956.

Hare, A. Paul *et al.* (eds.). *Small Groups.* New York: Alfred A. Knopf, 1955.

Harper, Floyd A. *Morals and the Welfare State.* Houghton-on-Hudson, N.Y.: Foundation for Economic Education, 1951.

Heilbroner, Robert L. *Quest for Wealth: A Study of Acquisitive Man.* New York: Simon & Schuster, 1956.

Herman, Abbott P. *An Approach to Social Problems.* New York: Ginn & Company, 1949.

Herrick, Virgil E. and Tyler, Ralph W. (eds.). *Toward Improved Curriculum Theory.* Chicago: University of Chicago Press, 1950.

Hertzler, Joyce O. *Social Institutions.* Lincoln: University of Nebraska Press, 1946.

Hickman, C. Addison and Kuhn, Manford H. *Individuals, Groups and Economic Behavior.* New York: The Dryden Press, 1956.

Hirsh, Selma. *The Fears Men Live By.* New York: Harper and Brothers, 1955.

Hogan, John D. and Ianni, F. A. J. *American Social Legislation.* New York: Harper and Brothers, 1956.

Hollis, Ernest V. and Taylor, Alice L. *Social Work Education in the United States.* New York: Columbia University Press, 1951.

Honsden, G. L. *Prevention of Cruelty to Children.* New York: The Philosophical Library, 1956.

Howard, Donald S. "Social Welfare" in *Encyclopedia Americana,* Volume 25, 1957.

Hoyt, Elizabeth E. *et al. American Income and Its Use.* New York: Harper and Brothers, 1954.

Hudson, J. W. "Recent Shifts in Ethical Theory and Practice," *Philosophical Review,* 49 (1940).

Hunter, Floyd. *Community Power Structure: A Study of Decision Makers.* Chapel Hill: University of North Carolina Press, 1953.

Hurst, Willard. *The Growth of American Law.* Boston: Little, Brown & Company, 1950.

Huxley, Julian. *New Bottles for New Wine: Ideology and Scientific Knowledge.* London: Royal Anthropological Institution of Great Britain and Ireland, 1950.

Isard, Walter and Whitney, V. H. *Atomic Power, An Economic and Social Analysis.* New York: The Blakiston Company, 1952.

Jacques, Elliott. *Measurement of Responsibility.* Cambridge: Harvard University Press, 1956.

Jahoda, Marie. *Current Concepts of Positive Mental Health.* New York: Joint Commission on Mental Illness and Health, 1958.

James, George. "Changing Priorities in Public Health," *Public Health Reports* (July 1956).

Jessop, Thomas E. *Social Ethics: Christian and Natural.* London: The Epworth Press, 1952.

Joesten, Joachim. *Vice Inc.* New York: Ace Books, 1954.

Johnson, Donald M. *Psychology of Thought and Judgment.* New York: Harper and Brothers, 1955.

Johnson, F. Ernest (ed). *Religion and Social Work.* New York: Harper and Brothers, 1956.

Kahn, Alfred. "Research Planning: Facilitating Social Work Research," *Social Service Review,* XXX (September 1956).

Kaplan, Morton A. *System and Process in International Politics.* New York: John Wiley & Sons, 1957.

Kasius, Cora (ed.). *New Directions in Social Work.* New York: Harper and Brothers, 1954.

Keith-Lucas, Alan. *Decisions About People in Need.* Chapel Hill: University of North Carolina Press, 1957.

Kelsen, Hans. *What Is Justice? Justice, Law and Politics in the Mirror of Science; Collected Essays.* Berkeley: University of California Press, 1957.

Kendall, Katherine A. "Education for Social Work" in *Social Work*

Year Book 1957. New York: National Association of Social Workers, 1957.

Key, V. O., Jr. *American State Politics: An Introduction*. New York: Alfred A. Knopf, 1956.

Klein, Philip. "The Social Theory of Professional Social Work" in Harry Elmer Barnes *et al., Contemporary Social Theory*. New York: Century, 1940.

Kluckhohn, Clyde and Murray, Henry A. (eds.). *Personality in Nature, Society and Culture*, 2nd ed. New York: Alfred A. Knopf, 1953.

Knight, Frank H. *Freedom and Reform*. New York: Harper and Brothers, 1947.

Landers, Paul. *Social Policies in the Making*. New York: D. C. Heath & Co., 1947.

Langer, Susanne K. *Philosophy in a New Key: A Study in the Symbolism of Reason, Rite and Art*. Cambridge: Harvard University Press, 1957.

Lash, Trude W. and Kahn, Alfred (eds.). *Children Absent from School*. New York: Citizens Committee on Children, 1949.

Lasswell, Harold D. *The Decision Process: Seven Categories of Functional Analysis*. College Park: University of Maryland, Bureau of Governmental Research, 1956.

Lee, Alfred McC. and Lee, E. B. (eds.). *Social Problems in America: A Source Book*. New York: Henry Holt and Company, 1949.

Lee, Dorothy D. "Are Basic Needs Ultimate?" in *Personality in Nature, Society and Culture*, ed. Clyde Kluckhohn and Henry A. Murray, 2nd ed. New York: Alfred A. Knopf, 1953.

Lee, Porter R. *Social Work: Cause and Function and Other Papers*. New York: Columbia University Press, 1937.

Lepley, Ray. *The Language of Value*. New York: Columbia University Press, 1957.

Lerner, Daniel and Lasswell, Harold D. (eds.). *The Policy Sciences: Recent Developments in Scope and Method*. Stanford, Calif.: Stanford University Press, 1951.

Levy, Marion J. *The Structure of Society*. Princeton: Princeton University Press, 1952.

Lewin, Kurt. *Resolving Social Conflicts*. New York: Harper and Brothers, 1948.

Lewis, Clarence I. *The Ground and Nature of the Right*. New York: Columbia University Press, 1955.

Leys, Wayne A. R. *Ethics for Policy Decisions*. New York: Prentice-Hall, 1952.

Lippitt, Ronald *et al. The Dynamics of Planned Change.* New York: Harcourt, Brace and Company, 1958.

Little, I. M. D. *A Critique of Welfare Economics.* Oxford: The Clarendon Press, 1950.

Los Angeles Welfare Planning Council Research Department. *A Conceptual Framework for the Study of Welfare Needs,* December 1956.

Lowenstein, Karl. *Political Power and the Governmental Process.* Chicago: University of Chicago Press, 1957.

Ludwig, Frederick J. *Youth and the Law.* Brooklyn, N.Y.: Foundation Press, 1955.

MacIver, Robert M. *Community: A Sociological Study.* New York: The Macmillan Company, 1924.

————. *Democracy and the Economic Challenge.* New York: Alfred A. Knopf, 1952.

————. "Government and Social Welfare" in *National Policies for Education, Health and Social Services,* ed. James E. Russell. Garden City, N.Y.: Doubleday and Company, 1955.

Marcus, Grace F. "The Responsibility of the Caseworker in the Conflict Between the Interests of the Individual and the Interests of Society" in *Proceedings of the National Conference of Social Work, 1940.* New York: Columbia University Press, 1940.

Martin, William O. *Order and Integration of Knowledge.* Ann Arbor: University of Michigan Press, 1957.

McKenny, Charles R. *Moral Problems in Social Work.* Milwaukee, Wis.: Bruce Publishing Company, 1951.

Meehl, Paul E. *Clinical versus Statistical Prediction.* Minneapolis: University of Minnesota Press, 1954.

Merrill, Francis E. "The Study of Social Problems" in *Analyzing Social Problems,* ed. John Eric Nordskog *et al.* New York: The Dryden Press, 1950.

Meyer, Agnes E. "No Man Is an Island," *Social Work,* 1 (July 1956).

Moneypenny, Philip. "The Control of Ethical Standards in the Public Service," *Annals of the American Academy of Political and Social Science,* Volume 297, 1955.

Morris, Albert. *Homicide: An Approach to the Problem of Crime.* Boston: Boston University Press, 1955.

Murphy, Arthur E. *The Uses of Reason.* New York: The Macmillan Company, 1943.

Myrdal, Alva. *Nation and Family: The Swedish Experiment in Demo-*

cratic Family and Population Policy. New York: Harper and Brothers, 1941.

Myrdal, Alva *et al. America's Role in International Social Welfare.* New York: Columbia University Press, 1955.

Myrdal, Gunnar. *An International Economy: Problems and Prospects.* New York: Harper and Brothers, 1957.

National Committee on Standards for the Professional Practice of Social Work. "Ethical Issues in Social Work," *Social Work Journal,* XXXVI (April 1955).

Nordskog, John Eric *et al.* (eds.). *Analyzing Social Problems.* New York: The Dryden Press, 1950.

Northrop, F. S. C. *Ideological Differences and World Order.* New Haven: Yale University Press, 1949.

Ogburn, William F. *Social Change.* New York: The Viking Press, 1950.

Ogle, Marbury B. *et al. Power, Order and the Economy.* New York: Harper and Brothers, 1954.

Ohlin, Lloyd E. *Sociology and the Field of Corrections.* New York: Russell Sage Foundation, 1956.

Olds, James. *The Growth and Structure of Motives.* Glencoe, Ill.: The Free Press, 1956.

Oliver, Henry M. *A Critique of Socioeconomic Goals.* Bloomington: Indiana University Press, 1954.

Parker, De Witt H. *Philosophy of Value.* Ann Arbor: University of Michigan Press, 1957.

Parsons, Talcott. *Essays in Sociological Theory, Pure and Applied,* rev. ed. Glencoe, Ill.: The Free Press, 1954.

Perlman, Helen H. *Social Casework: A Problem-Solving Process.* Chicago: University of Chicago Press, 1957.

Perloff, Harvey S. *Education for Planning.* Baltimore: Johns Hopkins University Press, 1957.

Pipping, Hugo E. *Standard of Living: The Concept and Its Place in Economics.* Helsinki: Societas Scientarum Fennica, 1953.

Polanyi, Karl. *The Great Transformation.* New York: Rinehart and Company, 1944.

Poole, Kenyon E. (ed.). *Fiscal Policies and the American Economy.* New York: Prentice-Hall, 1951.

Pray, Kenneth L. M. *Social Work in a Revolutionary Age, and Other Papers.* Philadelphia: University of Pennsylvania Press, 1949.

Rader, Melvin M. *Ethics and Society: An Appraisal of Social Ideals.* New York: Henry Holt and Company, 1950.

Robinson, D. H. *Vitality and All That.* New York: The Macmillan Company, 1952.

Ross, Murray G. *Community Organization: Theory and Principles.* New York: Harper and Brothers, 1955.

————. "Conceptual Problems in Community Organization," *Social Service Review,* XXX (June 1956).

Rowntree, B. Seebohm and Lavers, G. R. *Poverty and the Welfare State.* London: Longmans, Green & Company, 1951.

Russell, James E. (ed.). *National Policies for Education, Health and Social Services.* Garden City, N.Y.: Doubleday and Company, 1955.

Ryan, Thomas A. *Work and Effort.* New York: The Ronald Press, 1947.

Schubert, Glendon A., Jr. "The 'Public Interest' in Administrative Decision-Making: Theorem, Theosophy or Theory?", *American Political Science Review,* 51 (1957).

Selekman, Sylvia K. and Benjamin M. *Power and Morality in a Business Society.* New York: McGraw-Hill Book Company, 1956.

Seligman, Lester G. "The 'Public Policy' Orientation and the Social Science Course," *Journal of General Education* (January 1955).

Simon, Herbert A. *Administrative Behavior: A Study of the Decision-Making Processes in Administrative Organization,* 2nd ed. New York: The Macmillan Company, 1957.

Simpson, Sidney P. *et al. Cases and Readings on Law and Society.* St. Paul, Minn.: West Publishing Company, 1948–49.

Smith, A. Delafield. *The Right to Life.* Chapel Hill: University of North Carolina Press, 1957.

Sprout, Harold and Margaret. *Man-Milieu Relationship: Hypotheses in the Context of International Politics.* Princeton: Princeton University Center of International Studies, 1956.

Stein, Harold (ed.). *Public Administration and Policy Development.* New York: Harcourt, Brace and Company, 1952.

Stogdill, Ralph M. "Leadership, Membership and Organization," *Psychological Bulletin,* 47 (1950).

Stone, Julius. *The Province and Function of Law: Law as Logic, Justice and Social Control; A Study of Jurisprudence.* Toronto: Carswell Company, 1946.

Studt, Elliot. "The Contribution of Correctional Practice to Social Work Theory and Education," *Social Casework,* XXXVII (June 1956).

Sumner, William G. *Folkways.* New York: Ginn and Company, 1907.

Taylor, Donald W. and McNemar, Olga W. "Problem-Solving and Thinking," *Annual Review of Psychology,* 6 (1955).

Taylor, Paul S. "The Relation of Research to Legislative and Administrative Decisions," *Journal of Social Issues,* 3 (1947).

ten Broek, Jacobus and Wilson, Richard B. "Public Assistance and Social Insurance: A Normative Evaluation," University of California, Los Angeles, *Law Review* (April 1954).

Thomas, William L., Jr., et al. (eds.). *Man's Role in Changing the Face of the Earth.* Chicago: University of Chicago Press, 1956.

Titmuss, Richard M. *Problems of Social Policy.* New York: Longmans, Green & Company, 1950.

Towle, Charlotte. *Common Human Needs.* New York: American Association of Social Workers, 1952.

———. *The Learner in Education for the Professions.* Chicago: University of Chicago Press, 1954.

Truman, David B. *The Governmental Process.* New York: Alfred A. Knopf, 1951.

Tyler, Ralph W. *Basic Principles of Curriculum and Instruction.* Chicago: University of Chicago Press, 1950.

———. "Distinctive Attributes of Education for the Professions," *Social Work Journal,* XXXIII (April 1952).

——— et al. *Analysis of the Purpose, Pattern, Scope and Structure of the Officer Education Program of Air University.* Officer Education Research Laboratory. Maxwell Air Force Base, Alabama, May 1955.

United Nations. Department of Social Affairs. *Methods of Social Welfare Administration.* New York: Columbia University Press, 1955.

———. Department of Social Affairs. *Training for Social Work—An International Survey.* New York: Columbia University Press, 1950.

UNESCO. *Human Rights, Comments and Interpretations.* New York: Columbia University Press, 1949.

U.S. Commission on Intergovernmental Relations. *Federal Aid to Welfare.* Washington, D.C.: Government Printing Office, June 1955.

U.S. Congress. *Making Ends Meet on Less than $2,000 a Year.* Joint Senate-House Committee on the Economic Report, 82nd Congress, 1st Session. Washington, D.C.: Government Printing Office, 1951.

Waldo, Dwight (ed.). *Ideas and Issues in Public Administration.* New York: McGraw-Hill Book Company, 1953.

Warner, W. Lloyd et al. *Social Class in America.* Chicago: Science Research Associates, 1949.

Weber, Max. *The Theory of Social and Economic Organization,* tr. A. M. Henderson and Talcott Parsons. New York: Oxford University Press, 1947.

Weigert, Hans W. *Principles of Political Geography.* New York: Appleton-Century-Crofts, 1957.

White, Ralph G. *Value Analysis.* New York: Society for the Psychological Study of Social Issues, 1951.

White, R. K. "Ultimate and Near-Ultimate Democratic Values," *Progressive Education* (April 1950).

Whitehead, Alfred North. *The Aims of Education and Other Essays.* New York: The Macmillan Company, 1929.

Whyte, William H., Jr. *The Organization Man.* New York: Simon and Schuster, 1956.

Wickenden, Elizabeth. *How to Influence Public Policy.* New York: American Association of Social Workers, 1954.

Wiener, Norbert. *The Human Use of Human Beings: Cybernetics and Society.* Boston: Houghton Mifflin & Company, 1954.

Wilensky, Harold L. and Lebeaux, Charles N. *Industrial Society and Social Welfare.* New York: Russell Sage Foundation, 1958.

Witmer, Helen L. *Social Work: An Analysis of a Social Institution.* New York: Farrar and Rinehart, 1942.

—— and Kotinsky, Ruth (eds.). *Personality in the Making.* New York: Harper and Brothers, 1952.

—— and Tufts, Edith M. *The Effectiveness of Delinquency Prevention Programs.* U.S. Department of Health, Education, and Welfare, Children's Bureau. Washington, D.C.: U.S. Government Printing Office, 1954.

Wolins, Martin. *Social Welfare Problems and Services in Berkeley, California.* Berkeley: University of California School of Social Welfare, November 1954.

Wright, Helen R. "The Professional Curriculum of the Future," *Social Service Review,* XXV (December 1951).

Young, Donald. "Sociology and the Practicing Professions," *American Sociological Review,* XX (December 1955).

Younghusband, Eileen L. *Social Work in Britain; A Supplementary Report on the Employment and Training of Social Workers.* Edinburgh: T. and A. Constable, Ltd., 1951.

Younglich, Anita. *Dynamics of Social Interaction.* New York: Public Affairs Press, 1954.

Znaniecki, Florian. "Social Organization and Institutions" in *Twentieth Century Sociology,* ed. Georgil D. Gurvitch and Wilbert E. Moore. New York: The Philosophical Library, 1945.